First World War
and Army of Occupation
War Diary
France, Belgium and Germany

58 DIVISION
175 Infantry Brigade
London Regiment
2/10 Battalion
3 February 1917 - 31 March 1919

WO95/3009/5

The Naval & Military Press Ltd
www.nmarchive.com
Published in association with The National Archives

Published by

The Naval & Military Press Ltd

Unit 10 Ridgewood Industrial Park,

Uckfield, East Sussex,

TN22 5QE England

Tel: +44 (0) 1825 749494

www.naval-military-press.com

www.nmarchive.com

This diary has been reprinted in facsimile from the original. Any imperfections are inevitably reproduced and the quality may fall short of modern type and cartographic standards.

© **Crown Copyright**
Images reproduced by permission of The National Archives, London, England, 2015.

Contents

Document type	Place/Title	Date From	Date To
Miscellaneous	WO95/3009/5		
Heading	War Diary of 2/10th Bn London Regt. from Feb. 3rd 1917 to 26th Feb. 1917 (Volume 1)		
War Diary	Longbridge Deverill Wilts.	03/02/1917	04/02/1917
War Diary	Le Havre	05/02/1917	06/02/1917
War Diary	Abbeville	07/02/1917	07/02/1917
War Diary	Le Souich	08/02/1917	14/02/1917
War Diary	Trenches	15/02/1917	19/02/1917
War Diary	Gaudiempre	20/02/1917	20/02/1917
War Diary	Halloy	23/02/1917	23/02/1917
War Diary	Pommera	25/02/1917	26/02/1917
Miscellaneous	Marching Out State. 2/10th Battalion. The London Regiment.	04/02/1917	04/02/1917
Miscellaneous	Marching in State. 2/10th Battalion. The London Regiment.	08/02/1917	08/02/1917
Heading	War Diary of 2/10th Bn London Regt. from 27th Feb 1917 to 26th Mar 1917 (Volume 2)		
War Diary	Pommera	28/02/1917	28/02/1917
War Diary	Gaudiempre	01/03/1917	01/03/1917
War Diary	Riviere	04/03/1917	04/03/1917
War Diary	F.I.	05/03/1917	05/03/1917
War Diary	Sector F.I.	06/03/1917	13/03/1917
War Diary	Sub Sector FI	14/03/1917	26/03/1917
Heading	War Diary of 2/10th Bn London Regt From 27th March 1917 to 26th April 1917 (Volume 3)		
War Diary	Halloy	27/03/1917	31/03/1917
War Diary	Neuvillette	01/04/1917	01/04/1917
War Diary	Villers L'Hopital	02/04/1917	05/04/1917
War Diary	Bus-Les-Artois	06/04/1917	09/04/1917
War Diary	Miraumont.	10/04/1917	14/04/1917
War Diary	Acheit-Le-Petit	15/04/1917	26/04/1917
Heading	War Diary of 2/10 Bn London Regt From 27th April 1917 to 26th May. 1917 (Volume 4)		
War Diary	Acheit-Le-Petit.	27/04/1917	04/05/1917
War Diary	Ref. Sheet 57C N.W. I 4 B 88.	05/05/1917	12/05/1917
War Diary	Favreuil	13/05/1917	14/05/1917
War Diary	Bihucourt	15/05/1917	19/05/1917
War Diary	Mory	20/05/1917	21/05/1917
War Diary	Ecoust St Mien	22/05/1917	23/05/1917
War Diary	Ecoust	24/05/1917	26/05/1917
Heading	War Diary of 2/10th Battalion London Regt. From 27th May 1917 to 30th June 1917 (Volume 5)		
War Diary	Bullecourt	27/05/1917	29/05/1917
War Diary	Mory	30/05/1917	02/06/1917
War Diary	Ecoust	03/06/1917	06/06/1917
War Diary	Bullecourt	07/06/1917	14/06/1917
War Diary	Mory	15/06/1917	23/06/1917
War Diary	Logeast Wood	24/06/1917	25/06/1917
War Diary	Logeast	26/06/1917	30/06/1917

Heading	War Diary 2/10th Battn London Regt. From July 1st 1917 To July 31st 1917 Volume VI		
War Diary	Logeast	01/07/1917	04/07/1917
War Diary	Baricourt	05/07/1917	05/07/1917
War Diary	Ytres	06/07/1917	07/07/1917
War Diary	Havrincourt Wood	08/07/1917	26/07/1917
War Diary	Neuville	27/07/1917	27/07/1917
War Diary	Dainville	28/07/1917	31/07/1917
Miscellaneous	Report of a hostile raid on a sector of the line held by 2/10th London Regiment.	21/07/1917	21/07/1917
Miscellaneous	2/10th. Bn. London Regt.	25/07/1917	25/07/1917
Heading	War Diary of 2/10th Bn London Regt. From 1st Aug 1917-31st Aug 1917 (Volume 7)		
War Diary	Dainville	01/08/1917	31/08/1917
Heading	War Diary of 2/10th London Regt From 1st September 1917 30th September 1917 (Volume 8)		
War Diary	St Julien	31/08/1917	30/09/1917
Heading	War Diary 2/10th Battn London Regiment 1st October 1917 31st October 1917 (Volume 9)		
War Diary		01/10/1917	14/10/1917
War Diary	Nuile	15/10/1917	20/10/1917
War Diary	St Janter Biezen	21/10/1917	31/10/1917
Heading	War Diary 2/10th Battalion London Regiment From 1st Nov 1917 30th Nov 1917 (Volume 9)		
War Diary	Hanes Canal Bk	01/11/1917	07/11/1917
War Diary	In The Line	07/11/1917	08/11/1917
War Diary	Lige Camp	09/11/1917	14/11/1917
War Diary	Privete Camp	15/11/1917	30/11/1917
Heading	War Diary of 2/10 Bn London Regt. From 1st December 1917 to 31st December 1917 (Volume 11)		
War Diary	Bayenghem (Lombres Area)	01/12/1917	06/12/1917
War Diary	Siege Camp Elerd In Ghe	07/12/1917	07/12/1917
War Diary	Pollcabbelle Sector	08/12/1917	16/12/1917
War Diary	Canal Bank	17/12/1917	24/12/1917
War Diary	In The Line Poelcappelle & Langemarck Sector	24/12/1917	31/12/1917
Heading	War Diary of 2/10th London Regt From 1st January 1918 to 31st January 1918 Volume I		
War Diary	In The Line Laeqeimark	01/01/1918	01/01/1918
War Diary	Canal Bank	02/01/1918	07/01/1918
War Diary	Herzeele	08/01/1918	20/01/1918
War Diary	Villers Bretonneaux	21/01/1918	21/01/1918
War Diary	Fouilloy	22/01/1918	05/02/1918
War Diary	Bois De Vieville	06/02/1918	07/02/1918
War Diary	Line	08/02/1918	22/02/1918
War Diary	Bois De Vieville	23/02/1918	28/02/1918
Heading	War Diary 2/10th London Regt Volume III March 1st 31st 1918		
War Diary	Beittes de Roug	01/03/1918	09/03/1918
War Diary	Liue	10/03/1918	29/03/1918
War Diary	Preircuaude	30/03/1918	31/03/1918
Heading	175th Inf. Bde. 58th Div. War Diary 2/10th Battn. The London Regiment. April 1918		
Heading	War Diary 2/10th London Volume II April 1918		
War Diary	Buttes De Rouy	01/04/1918	02/04/1918
War Diary	Pereeuraude	03/04/1918	03/04/1918
War Diary	Lauiceuies	04/04/1918	05/04/1918

War Diary	Haugcan	06/04/1918	06/04/1918
War Diary	Liue Billets	07/04/1918	07/04/1918
War Diary	Bretonneux	08/04/1918	09/04/1918
War Diary	Villers Bretonneux	10/04/1918	23/04/1918
War Diary	Line Haugard Sector	24/04/1918	30/04/1918
Heading	War Diary 2/10th London Regt Volume V May 1918		
War Diary	Line	15/05/1918	16/05/1918
War Diary	Front Line	17/05/1918	22/05/1918
War Diary	Henencourt Wood	23/05/1918	31/05/1918
War Diary	Ailly Le Haut Clocher	01/05/1918	06/05/1918
War Diary	Bazieux	07/05/1918	08/05/1918
War Diary	Line	09/05/1918	15/05/1918
Miscellaneous	The Hairpin-Albert.		
Miscellaneous	2/10th London Regiment.	18/05/1918	18/05/1918
Miscellaneous	2/10th London Regiment.	20/05/1918	20/05/1918
Miscellaneous	2/10th London Regiment. Relief Orders. Evening 22nd May 1918	22/05/1918	22/05/1918
Miscellaneous	2/10th London Regiment Millencourt Sector.		
Miscellaneous	Midnight 27/28/May. E.P. 104	27/05/1918	27/05/1918
Miscellaneous	Headquarters. 175th Infantry Brigade. E.P. 106	28/05/1918	28/05/1918
Miscellaneous	Headquarters. 175th Infantry Brigade. E.P. 112	29/05/1918	29/05/1918
Miscellaneous	To all Companies. 2/10th Londons E.P. 115	30/05/1918	30/05/1918
Miscellaneous	E.P. 121	30/05/1918	30/05/1918
Miscellaneous	Millencourt Sector Support Battalion Handing over statement 2/10th Londons to 8th East Surreys	31/05/1918	31/05/1918
Heading	2/10th Bn London Regt. War Diary From 1st June to 30th June 1918		
War Diary	Beheucourt	01/06/1918	04/06/1918
War Diary	Malkeus Aux Moors	05/06/1918	10/06/1918
War Diary	Briquemesnil.	11/06/1918	18/06/1918
War Diary	Line	19/06/1918	23/06/1918
War Diary	Line Front Line	24/06/1918	30/06/1918
Heading	War Diary 2/10th London Regt Volume VII July 1st 31st 1918		
War Diary	Line	01/07/1918	06/07/1918
War Diary	Baizieux System	07/07/1918	12/07/1918
War Diary	Front Line	12/07/1918	16/07/1918
War Diary	Support Line	17/07/1918	19/07/1918
War Diary	Front	20/07/1918	29/07/1918
War Diary	Line	30/07/1918	31/07/1918
Heading	175th Bde. 58th Div. 2/10th Battalion The London Regiment August 1918		
Heading	War Diary Volume VIII August 1st August 31st 1918 2/10th London Regt		
War Diary		01/08/1918	07/08/1918
War Diary	Line	08/08/1918	22/08/1918
War Diary	Support Line	23/08/1918	25/08/1918
War Diary	Line	25/08/1918	31/08/1918
Heading	2/10th Battalion, The London Regiment. Summary of Operations. Bailly-Laurette and Chipilly August 3rd to 12th 1918		
Miscellaneous	2/10th Battalion, London Regiment.		
Miscellaneous	Phase 2 Advance Towards Chipilly		
Miscellaneous	Third Phase The Capture of Chipilly Spur		
Map	Map B		
Map	Map C		

Map	Map D		
Map	Map E		
Miscellaneous			
Miscellaneous		21/08/1918	21/08/1918
Heading	2/10th, Battalion The London Regiment. Summary of Operations. Sailly-Laurette and Chipilly August to 1918		
Miscellaneous	The Battalion Orders for the Capture of Sailly Laurette	07/08/1918	07/08/1918
Miscellaneous	Supplement to Order for capture of Sailly Laurette		
Miscellaneous		21/08/1918	21/08/1918
War Diary		01/09/1918	06/09/1918
War Diary	Line	07/09/1918	30/09/1918
War Diary	Lievin	01/10/1918	07/10/1918
War Diary	Line	08/10/1918	13/10/1918
War Diary	Map Sheet 44A	14/10/1918	18/10/1918
War Diary	Map Sheet 44	19/10/1918	30/11/1918
War Diary	Stambruges	01/12/1918	20/12/1918
War Diary	Leuze	21/12/1918	28/02/1919
Miscellaneous		31/03/1919	31/03/1919
War Diary	Leuze	01/03/1919	31/03/1919

30 95
3009/5

WAR DIARY or INTELLIGENCE SUMMARY.

(Erase heading not required.)

Army Form C. 2118.

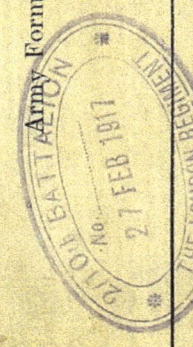

Vol 1

CONFIDENTIAL

WAR DIARY

of

2/10th Bn LONDON REGT.

from Feb. 3rd 1917 to 26th Feb 1917

(Volume 1)

Army Form C. 2118.

WAR DIARY
or
INTELLIGENCE SUMMARY.
(Erase heading not required.)

Instructions regarding War Diaries and Intelligence Summaries are contained in F. S. Regs., Part II. and the Staff Manual respectively. Title pages will be prepared in manuscript.

Place	Date	Hour	Summary of Events and Information	Remarks and references to Appendices
Longbridge Deverill WILTS.	1914 Feb. 3rd	10.23 pm	Advised to move on Feb. 4th as follows:— Train. X.171 Dep WARMINSTER. 5.50 am. do. X.172 Dep do. 7.0 am	JMcC
	Feb. 4th	5.30 am	Left WARMINSTER as follows:— X.171. 5.30am. X.172. 6.30am. Marching Out State attached.	(1)
			Arrived SOUTHAMPTON 7.35am and 8.45 am.	
		4.10pm	Left SOUTHAMPTON 4.10 pm per S.S. ARCHANGEL.	
		11.0pm	Arrived LE HAVRE 11.0 pm and disembarked.	JMcC
LE HAVRE	Feb 5th	4.50 am	Arrived at No 1 Rest Camp. LE HAVRE.	
		11.0	Received orders to leave Rest Camp at 6.30 am on the 6th leaving	
		pm	9 Officers & 300 men to follow at 5.30 pm.	JMcC
LE HAVRE	Feb. 6th	2.30 pm	Entrained at POINT 3 and left LE HAVRE for ABBEVILLE to receive further instructions there as to Detraining Station	JMcC

T2134. Wt. W708—776. 500000. 4/15. Sir J. C. & S.

WAR DIARY
or
INTELLIGENCE SUMMARY.
(Erase heading not required.)

Army Form C. 2118.

Place	Date	Hour	Summary of Events and Information	Remarks and references to Appendices
ABBEVILLE	7/2/17	7.45 a.m.	Received orders to entrain at AUXI-LE-CHATEAU.	
		9.10 a.m.	Left.	
		11.50 a.m.	Arrived AUXI-LE-CHATEAU and detrained.	
		2.15 p.m.	Left AUXI-LE-CHATEAU by motor lorries for LE SOUICH.	
		3.15 p.m.	Arrived LE SOUICH and occupied billets marching in state attached.	(2)
LE SOUICH	8/2/17	7.0 a.m.	Remainder of Battn. (9 Offrs & 300 O.R.) arrived via ABBEVILLE and FREVENT.	
LE SOUICH	12/2/17	8.5 a.m.	Received orders to prepare to move on 14/2/17 to be attached for instruction to 148th Inf. Bde, transport to remain at LE SOUICH.	
LE SOUICH	13/2/17	9.15 a.m.	Received orders to move on 14th inst. to LA CAUCHIE by bus; thence to be attached to 148th Inf. Bde for instruction; Transport to proceed to BAILLEULMONT.	

WAR DIARY
or
INTELLIGENCE SUMMARY.
(Erase heading not required.)

Army Form C. 2118.

Place	Date	Hour	Summary of Events and Information	Remarks and references to Appendices
LE SOUICH	14/4/17	10.15 a.m.	Left LE SOUICH for LA CAUCHIE via DOULLENS – POMMERA – LAHERLIERE. Thence split up by Companies for instruction under 148th Bde. as follows:- H.Q. to 1/5th K.O.Y.L.I. in trenches B. Coy to do A. Coy to 1/4th do BELLACOURT. C. Coy to 1/4th YORKS + LANCS in trenches D. Coy to 1/5th K.O.Y.L.I. at BAILLEULVAL + BASSEUX. No casualties	
Trenches	15/4/17		Casualties four killed, two wounded (one slightly) shell fire, one accidentally shot + died of wounds.	
Trenches	16/4/17		A Coy relieved C Coy (as above) and D. Coy relieved B. Coy. No casualties.	

Army Form C. 2118.

WAR DIARY
or
INTELLIGENCE SUMMARY.
(Erase heading not required.)

Instructions regarding War Diaries and Intelligence Summaries are contained in F.S. Regs., Part II. and the Staff Manual respectively. Title pages will be prepared in manuscript.

Place	Date	Hour	Summary of Events and Information	Remarks and references to Appendices
Trenches	19/2/17	—	Attachment to 148th Bde. ceased. Proceeded to CAUDIEMPRÉ and occupied billets there at 2.0 p.m.	
CAUDIEMPRE	20/2/17	7.30 a.m.	Left CAUDIEMPRE & proceeded to HALLOY via PAS and occupied billets.	
HALLOY	23/2/17	10.0 a.m.	Left HALLOY & proceeded to POMMERA and occupied billets.	
POMMERA	25/2/17	1.20 a.m.	Arrived of indications of retirement of enemy opposite 5 Corps on our right. To be ready to move by 5.0 a.m.	
POMMERA	26/2/17		Received orders to proceed to CAUDIEMPRÉ on 28/2/17; thence to RIVIERE on 1/3/17 to occupy Reserve Billets both are to lay in "Keeps".	

Vaurobosch Lt/Col
2/10th [illegible]

T2134. Wt. W708—776. 500000. 4/15. Sir J. C. & S.

MARCHING OUT STATE.

2/10th Battalion, The London Regiment.

LONGBRIDGE DEVERILL.

4th February, 1917.

DISTRIBUTION.	Officers.	Warrant Officers.	Sergeants.	Lance-Sergeants.	Corporals.	Lance-Corporals.	Privates.	Total, W.O's, N.C.O's and Men.	HORSES. Riding.	Draught.	Pack.	Total.	VEHICLES. 2-wheeled wagons.	4-wheeled wagons.	Bicycles.
(1) Proceeding overseas with 2/10th Battalion, The London Regiment:—															
(a). On Battalion Strength.	34	6	40	20	33	61	782	942	12	34	9	55	4	17	10
(b). Attached.	1	-	1	-	2	1	9	13	2	8	-	10			
(c). Supernumerary (O.R.Sgt)			1					1							
(d). Total proceeding overseas with unit	35	6	42	20	35	62	791	956	14	42	9	65	4	17	10.
(2) Already proceeded overseas ...	2	-	-	-	-	-	2	2	-	-	-	-	-	-	-
(3) TOTAL PROCEEDING OVERSEAS. ...	37	6	42	20	35	62	793	958	14	42	9	65	4	17	10.

J. Mittell
for O.C. 2/10th Battalion
Lieut Adjt. London Regt.

MARCHING IN STATE.

2/10th Battalion. The London Regiment.

8-2-17.

DISTRIBUTION.	Officers.	Warrant Officers.	Sergeants.	Lance Sergeants	Corporals.	Lance Corporals.	Privates.	Total W.O.'s N.C.O.'s & men	HORSES Riding.	Draught.	Pack.	VEHICLES Two wheeled	Four wheeled	Bicycles.
Proceeded overseas with unit :-														
(a) On Battalion Strength	34	6	40	20	33	61	779	939	12	34	9	4	17	10
(b) Attached	1		1		2	1	9	13	2	8	-			
T O T A L	35	6	41	20	35	62	788	952	14	42	9	4	17	10

J. Metcalf
Lieut. & Adjt.
For O.C. 2/10th Battalion.
The London Regiment.

8-2-17.

Army Form C. 2118.

WAR DIARY
or
INTELLIGENCE SUMMARY.

(Erase heading not required.)

Vol 2

CONFIDENTIAL.

WAR DIARY

of

2/10th Bn LONDON REGT.

FROM 27th Feb. 1917 to 26th Mar. 1917.

(Volume 2)

WAR DIARY
INTELLIGENCE SUMMARY.
(Erase heading not required.)

Army Form C. 2118.

Place	Date	Hour	Summary of Events and Information	Remarks and references to Appendices
POMMERA	28/2/17	10.15 am	Moved to GAUDIEMPRE & occupied billets.	
GAUDIEMPRE	1/3/17	7.0 pm	Moved to RIVIERE to occupy Reserve Billets. Distribution:- A.B.&C. to billets, D Coy in keeps at SUGAR FACTORY, PETIT MOULIN KEEP, WAILLY KEEP & PETIT CHATEAU KEEP.	
RIVIERE	4/3/17	3.0 p	Relieved 2/9 London Regt. in the trenches (Sector F.1.). Relief complete by 3.0 pm. Situation normal. Some shelling from Minenwerfers throughout afternoon & evening but no casualties. Gas Alarm at 7.45 pm but only a few gas shells over.	
F.1.	5/3/17		Situation normal. Heavy shelling by Minenwerfers on our right flank in vicinity of MARTINET'S WOOD. Our support line shelled during the evening — a few gas shells over. No casualties. Gas Alarm 7.45 pm but no Gas. Gas Plat. of D. Coy took over SUGAR FACTORY KEEP & WAILLY KEEP.	

WAR DIARY
or
INTELLIGENCE SUMMARY.
(Erase heading not required.)

Army Form C. 2118.

Place	Date	Hour	Summary of Events and Information	Remarks and references to Appendices
SECTOR F.1.	6/3/17		Situation quieter & Artillery shelling slight except between 2.30 – 3.30 p.m. on our right flank. Aerial activity throughout the day. FOREST ST. (O.T.) badly damaged by MINENWERFER. Casualties - 1 slightly wounded.	JWh
ditto.	7.3.17		Unusually quiet except for Machine Guns & Snipers. Gas Alarm 5.0 a.m. but no Gas. Casualties Nil.	JWh
ditto	8.3.17		Again very quiet except between 4.5 & 4.45 a.m. when 33 Minnenwerfers fell around R.29.b & 45.90. M.G. & Snipers very active. Patrol sent out at 10.0 p.m. found enemy at work on Sep.26. Very little patrolling possible owing to brilliant moonlight. No casualties	JWh

WAR DIARY
or
INTELLIGENCE SUMMARY.
(Erase heading not required.)

Army Form C. 2118.

Place	Date	Hour	Summary of Events and Information	Remarks and references to Appendices
SECTOR F1	9.3.17		Enemy artillery & trench mortars very active during the day. During most of the afternoon our Support & Reserve lines were shelled. Some 5.9 shells being put over. Our own artillery was active & our aeroplanes were over enemy lines.	JSP
	10.3.17		Enemy M.G's & Snipers active. Trench mortars fairly active. Rifle Grenades & rifle bombs continuously fired on our trenches. Enemy artillery fairly active - between 6.15 & 7.30 P.M. two shrapnel burst over our Reserve lines & again between 5 & 6.30 P.M. Our artillery retour apparently shelling enemy back areas. Our T.M's fired in direction of BEAIRVILLE WOOD between 3.45 & 5 P.M. Our patrols active in no-mans-land & examining enemy saps.	JSP
	11.3.17		Enemy M.G's busy during night. L.T.M's at intervals during the day. Rifle grenades & some 5.9 shells, falling at R.29.a.70.50. Enemy artillery active. Sn.? shrapnel shells on our support & reserve lines & our villages & back areas were shelled during the morning. Enemy aircraft very active. Our own artillery & aircraft active. Casualty one man wounded.	JSP

Army Form C. 2118.

WAR DIARY
or
INTELLIGENCE SUMMARY.
(Erase heading not required.)

Instructions regarding War Diaries and Intelligence Summaries are contained in F.S. Regs., Part II. and the Staff Manual respectively. Title pages will be prepared in manuscript.

Place	Date	Hour	Summary of Events and Information	Remarks and references to Appendices
SECTOR F1	12.3.17		Enemy T.M.s at 7 A.M. fired a number of shells on FOREST STREET C.T. Nine T.M. bombs were dropped on our post No. 5. R.29.a.30.10 between 4.30 & 5 P.M. Ten rifle grenades at same spot in the evening. Sniper active. Enemy aircraft active between 4 & 6 P.M. Enemy artillery active against our back areas, several gas shells dropped near Bn. H.Q. at 1.45 P.M. & shrapnel over front line place at 10.30 P.M. Our artillery retire. Sudden thaw & some rain caused front dilapidation in trenches. FINE STREET C.T. complete blocked. Our patrols active. Casualty. One man wounded.	
	13.3.17		Our artillery engaged in cutting gaps in Enemy wire. At 7.15 P.M. our artillery put a barrage on Enemy line at R.29.d.10.40 over 200 yds & a pty of 1 officer & 20 O.R. went over to reconnoitre a raid. The Enemy trenches were found to be very strongly manned by [illegible] & were evidently very good troops. Search lights & very lights made no man's land as light as day & a heavy & effective fire of rifles & M.G. grenades was maintained on our trenches. Enemy artillery reply not so effective. The raiding pty got back without casualties but lost three men wounded in fire trench. Casualties two officers & one man killed, two officers and six men wounded.	*1 2/Lt. H.D. KING 2/Lt. J. CURRIE *2. LT. HADY. A.N. NETTELL LT. B. REV. HARDCASTLE

Army Form C. 2118.

WAR DIARY
or
INTELLIGENCE SUMMARY.
(Erase heading not required.)

Instructions regarding War Diaries and Intelligence Summaries are contained in F.S. Regs., Part II. and the Staff Manual respectively. Title pages will be prepared in manuscript.

Place	Date	Hour	Summary of Events and Information	Remarks and references to Appendices
Sub Sector F1	14.3.17		A normal amount of artillery activity on both sides. Fire from enemy field rifles on left of sub sector very effective covering practically all the ground from the front to behind Reserve line. Casualty one man killed	FSD
	15.3.17		Enemy artillery fairly active, many fine indiscriminates on many targets both in and behind our lines. Our aeroplanes & observation balloons active. Casualty One man wounded	FSD
	16.3.17		Enemy again distributed his artillery fire over many targets forming a limited number of rounds at each target. A very quiet day on his part, but his snipers & fixed rifles were as busy as usual and prevented any going on the top on our part, both by night & day, to get out of the trenches but C.T.s. Our artillery fire was mostly on back areas. Casualty one wounded	FSD
	17.3.17		Enemy very quiet all day. One of his planes, flying very high, got well over our back areas. Our planes active. Our guns fired on back areas	FSD

T/134. Wt. W708—776. 500000. 4/15. Sir J. C. & S.

WAR DIARY or INTELLIGENCE SUMMARY.

Army Form C. 2118.

(Erase heading not required.)

Instructions regarding War Diaries and Intelligence Summaries are contained in F. S. Regs., Part II. and the Staff Manual respectively. Title pages will be prepared in manuscript.

Place	Date	Hour	Summary of Events and Information	Remarks and references to Appendices
Sub-Sector F1	18.3.17		During the night 17-18 March our patrols reported enemy front trench empty. Explosions and fires behind Enemy trenches had previously been noticed. At dawn "B" Company entered the Enemy's lines followed by the remainder of the Bn. Some shots were fired at them in the semi darkness coming from two Companies during the following night one Company was pushed forward to form an outpost line E of FICHEUX. Casualties one killed one wounded.	73f
	19.3.17		The Bn moved at 6.30 A.M. to take up an outpost line on the ARRAS-BAPAUME Road between BOIRY-BECQUERELLE and MERCATEL. The advance was opposed by small bodies of the Enemy, probably picket troops, judging by the way they fought — with machine guns & supported by two or three batteries of artillery at long range. M.G's fired upon us from BOIRY-BECQUERELLE & from N of HENIN-SUR-COJEUL. Artillery fire was fairly heavy & well placed as the Bn reached its objective & pushed out outposts. Enemy snipers were busy & skilful at intervals up to 10.30 P.M. The Enemy shelled our line. The Bn was relieved at 6.45 A.M. on 20th. Casualties three killed two wounded.	73f

Army Form C. 2118.

WAR DIARY
or
INTELLIGENCE SUMMARY.
(Erase heading not required.)

Instructions regarding War Diaries and Intelligence Summaries are contained in F.S. Regs., Part II. and the Staff Manual respectively. Title pages will be prepared in manuscript.

Place	Date	Hour	Summary of Events and Information	Remarks and references to Appendices
Sub Sector F1	20.3.17		The Bn was relieved at 6.45 A.M. and marched back to billets at Bellacourt after suffering one casualty from M.G. fire. Casualties one killed	J.3.1
	21.3.17		In billets at Bellacourt cleaning up, bathing, inspecting arms and equipment &c after sixteen successive days in the trenches	J.3.1
	22.3.17		Moved into billets at BERLES-AUX-BOIS	J.3.1
	23.3.17		Road mending at MONCHEY	J.3.1
	24.3.17		Platoon training at BERLES-AUX-BOIS	J.3.1
	25.3.17		Moved to HALLOY	J.3.1
	26.3.17		Platoon training & refitting at Halloy	J.3.1

Vaughan Lt.Col.
2/10th London Regt.

Army Form C. 2118.

WAR DIARY
or
INTELLIGENCE SUMMARY.
(Erase heading not required.)

Vol 3

CONFIDENTIAL

WAR DIARY

of

2/10th Bn LONDON REGT

From 27th March 1917 to 28th April 1917.

(Volume 3)

Army Form C. 2118.

WAR DIARY
INTELLIGENCE SUMMARY.
(Erase heading not required.)

Instructions regarding War Diaries and Intelligence Summaries are contained in F. S. Regs., Part II. and the Staff Manual respectively. Title pages will be prepared in manuscript.

Place	Date	Hour	Summary of Events and Information	Remarks and references to Appendices
HALLOY	27.3.17		Training & refitting	F.S.L
"	28.3.17		Training & refitting	F.S.L
"	29.3.17		Training & refitting	F.S.L
"	30.3.17		Training & refitting	F.S.L
"	31.3.17		Training & refitting	108
NEUVILLETTE	1.4.17		Moved into billets at NEUVILLETTE	109
VILLERS L'HOPITAL	2.4.17		Moved into billets at VILLERS L'HOPITAL	109
"	3.4.17		Training & refitting	108

WAR DIARY
INTELLIGENCE SUMMARY.
(Erase heading not required.)

Army Form C. 2118.

Instructions regarding War Diaries and Intelligence Summaries are contained in F. S. Regs., Part II. and the Staff Manual respectively. Title pages will be prepared in manuscript.

Place	Date	Hour	Summary of Events and Information	Remarks and references to Appendices
VILLERS L'HOPITAL	4.4.17.		Training & refitting continued.	NB
"	5.4.17.		'A' Coy & an extreme party from each company embussed at HERMIN EN on the PONT-LE-CHATEAU – VACQUERIE ROAD & were conveyed to BUS-LES-ARTOIS.	NB
BUS-LES-ARTOIS	6.4.17.		Remainder of Bn embussed at MAMUR EN & went into camp at BUS-LES-ARTOIS.	NB
"	7.4.17.		Bn acted as a working party to work under 275th A.T. Coy R.E.S.	NB
"	8.4.17.		Training & refitting	NB
"	9.4.17.		Moved into camp at MIRAUMONT.	NB
MIRAUMONT	10.4.17.		Bn acted as a working party on railway work under CANADIAN Rly Construction Coy. MAJOR T.O.R. MAIN accidentally injured.	NB

Army Form C. 2118.

WAR DIARY
INTELLIGENCE SUMMARY.
(Erase heading not required.)

Instructions regarding War Diaries and Intelligence Summaries are contained in F. S. Regs., Part II. and the Staff Manual respectively. Title pages will be prepared in manuscript.

Place	Date	Hour	Summary of Events and Information	Remarks and references to Appendices
MIRAUMONT	11.4.17		Bn employed as a working party under CANADIAN RLY COY.	W.D.
"	12.4.17		Bn employed as a working party	W.D.
"	13.4.17		Bn employed as a working party under CANADIAN RLY COY.	W.D.
"	14.4.17		Bn moves into huts at ACHEUX-LE-PETIT	W.D.
ACHEUX-LE-PETIT	15.4.17		Bn employed on working party.	W.D.
"	16.4.17		Bn employed on working party.	W.D.
"	17.4.17		Bn employed on various working parties.	W.D.
"	18.4.17		Bn employed on various working parties.	W.D.

WAR DIARY
INTELLIGENCE SUMMARY
(Erase heading not required.)

Army Form C. 2118.

Instructions regarding War Diaries and Intelligence Summaries are contained in F. S. Regs., Part II. and the Staff Manual respectively. Title pages will be prepared in manuscript.

Place	Date	Hour	Summary of Events and Information	Remarks and references to Appendices
ATHIES	19.4.17		Bn employed on covering working parties.	WD
"	20.4.17		Training continued.	WD
"	21.4.17		Bn employed on covering working parties.	WD
"	22.4.17		Bn employed on covering working parties.	WD
"	23.4.17		Training continued.	WD
"	24.4.17		Training continued.	WD
"	25.4.17		Rt-half Batt. employed on working party. Left half Bn continued training.	WD
"	26.4.17		Rt-half Bn employed on working party. Left half Bn continued training.	WD

J. Fountney Lt. Col. C.
2/16 Bn London Regt.

Army Form C. 2118.

WAR DIARY
INTELLIGENCE SUMMARY.
(Erase heading not required.)

175/58. Vol 4

CONFIDENTIAL

WAR DIARY

of

2/10 Bn LONDON REGT.

from 27th APRIL 1917 to 26th MAY 1917.

(Volume 4)

Army Form C. 2118.

WAR DIARY
or
INTELLIGENCE SUMMARY.
(Erase heading not required.)

Instructions regarding War Diaries and Intelligence Summaries are contained in F.S. Regs., Part II. and the Staff Manual respectively. Title pages will be prepared in manuscript.

Place	Date	Hour	Summary of Events and Information	Remarks and references to Appendices
ACHEUX-EN-AMIENS	27/4/17		Training continued	
"	28.4.17		Bn employed on various working parties	W.D.
"	29.4.17		Bn employed on various working parties	W.D.
"	30.4.17		Training continued	W.D.
A	1.5.17		Bn employed on various working parties	W.D.
"	2.5.17		Bn employed on various working parties	W.D.
"	3.5.17		Training continued	W.D.
"	4.5.17		Recd orders to camp at FAVREUIL vacated by 2nd ANZAC Division	W.D.

Army Form C. 2118.

WAR DIARY
INTELLIGENCE SUMMARY.
(Erase heading not required.)

Place	Date	Hour	Summary of Events and Information	Remarks and references to Appendices
M⁷ ⁵⁄₆ N.W.				
T.4.b.88.	5.5.17		Bn moved up to secure line S. of LAGNICOURT & relieved 2/1st Bn. Relief completed at 9.55 P.M.	W/D
do	6.5.17.		Situation normal.	W/D
do	7.5.17.		Situation normal. Zero at T4 & 68 shelled heavily during evening. S.O.S. answered.	W/D
do	8.5.17		Situation normal.	W/D
do	9.5.17		Situation normal. 9/12 Bn relieves 2/12 Bn in line (Left sector of Brigade line at LAGNICOURT. Relief completed 1.5 a.m. 10/5/17	W/D
	10/5/17		Situation normal. 2 O.R. wounded.	W/D

WAR DIARY
INTELLIGENCE SUMMARY

Army Form C. 2118.

Place	Date	Hour	Summary of Events and Information	Remarks and references to Appendices
	11.5.17		Situation normal. 3 O.R. killed + 13 O.R. wounded	W.S.L
	12.5.17		Situation normal. Bn relieved by 32nd Bn. Austr. Inf. and went into camp at FAVREUIL. Relief completed 12.30 am 13/5/17 — 3 O.R. killed Lieut C.A. STRITE and 7 O.R. gassed by shell gas 6 O.R. wounded.	W.S.L
FAVREUIL	13.5.17		Bn refitting.	W.S.L
	14.5.17		Bn training and re-fitting.	W.S.L
BIHUCOURT	15.5.17		Bn moved to BIHUCOURT and went into camp.	W.S.L
	16/5/17		Bn at training	W.S.L
	17/5/17		Bn at training	W.S.L

WAR DIARY
or
INTELLIGENCE SUMMARY.
(Erase heading not required.)

Army Form C. 2118.

Place	Date	Hour	Summary of Events and Information	Remarks and references to Appendices
BIHUCOURT	18/5/17		Bn. H.Q. conference at working parties. C.D. Company put through medical parade. Lt/Col. J.K. SULLIVAN, M.C., wards commanding and left for HAVRE.	
	19/5/17		Bn at training.	WSJ
MORY	20/5/17		Bn moved into camp at MORY.	WSJ
	21/5/17		Bn. at training and making camp.	WSJ
ECOUST St MIEN	22/5/17		Bn moved into ECOUST St MIEN in relief of 2/6th Bn West Regt and in support of 2/7 Bn. Relief completed 12.10 am 23/5/17. No casualties.	WSJ
	23/5/17		Bn remained at ECOUST.	WSJ

Army Form C. 2118.

WAR DIARY
or
INTELLIGENCE SUMMARY.
(Erase heading not required.)

Instructions regarding War Diaries and Intelligence Summaries are contained in F. S. Regs., Part II. and the Staff Manual respectively. Title pages will be prepared in manuscript.

Place	Date	Hour	Summary of Events and Information	Remarks and references to Appendices
ECOUST	24/5/17		300 men at work on right sector	655 J.
	25/5/17		400 men at work on right sector. Casualties 1/K killed 3 wounded	OR 652.
	26/5/17		Bn. relieved 2/9 Bn. in left sector. Relief complete 12.30 a.m. Casualties 1 OR wounded	105 J

J S Plowdrey
Major.
Commanding 4/6 Bn Yorks Regt.

Army Form C. 2118.

WAR DIARY
or
INTELLIGENCE SUMMARY.
(Erase heading not required.)

Vol 5

CONFIDENTIAL.

WAR DIARY

— of —

2/10th Battalion, London Regt.

from 27th May 1917 to 30th June 1917

(VOLUME 5.)

WAR DIARY
or
INTELLIGENCE SUMMARY.
(Erase heading not required.)

Army Form C. 2118.

Place	Date	Hour	Summary of Events and Information	Remarks and references to Appendices
BULLECOURT	27/5/17		Situation normal. Considerable shelling of village during night of 27/28 May. Casualties 6 O.R. killed 24 O.R. wounded.	WSJ
	28/5/17		Situation normal. Casualties 2/Lt I.R.G.T. Chapman (shell shock) and 3 O.R. wounded.	WSJ
	29/5/17		Situation normal. Bn. relieved by 2/7 Bn Durs Regt. Relief complete 2 am 30/5/17. Casualties 2 O.R. killed 10 O.R. wounded.	WSJ
MORY	30/5/17		Bn. went into camp at B 30 a at about 3 am & moved into camp at MORY during afternoon.	WSJ
	31/5/17		Bn. resting.	WSJ
	1/6/17		Bn. training and refitting. Lt.Col. L.W. SADLER-JACKSON, C.M.G., D.S.O. assumed command of the Bn. vice Lt.Col. G.K. SULLIVAN M.C.	WSJ

WAR DIARY
or
INTELLIGENCE SUMMARY.

(Erase heading not required.)

Army Form C. 2118.

Place	Date	Hour	Summary of Events and Information	Remarks and references to Appendices
MORY	2/9/17		Bn employed on working parties and at training	Les J.
ECOUST	3/9/17	12.30 am 4/9/17	Bn relieved 2/7 West London Regt. in left support position. Relief complete	Les J.
	4/9/17		Bn at ECOUST employed on working parties. 2/Lt J. TYNDALL killed by a shell. (19th London Regt attached to Bn.)	Les J.
	5/9/17		Bn at ECOUST employed on working parties. Casualties 2 O.R. wounded.	Les J.
	6/9/17		Bn employed on working parties. Casualties 1 OR wounded.	Les J.
	7/9/17	1.25 am 8/9/17	Bn relieves 2/3 Bn in line (left sector). Relief complete. Casualties: Lieut E.W. PULLEN wounded.	
BULLECOURT				

Army Form C. 2118.

WAR DIARY
or
INTELLIGENCE SUMMARY.
(Erase heading not required.)

Instructions regarding War Diaries and Intelligence Summaries are contained in F. S. Regs., Part II. and the Staff Manual respectively. Title pages will be prepared in manuscript.

Place	Date	Hour	Summary of Events and Information	Remarks and references to Appendices
BULLECOURT	8/6/17		Situation normal. Slight shelling at intervals. 2/Lt J. W. McGRATH wounded in throat by a sniper.	AS/.
	9/6/17		Situation normal and very quiet. No casualties.	AS/.
	10/6/17		Situation normal. Completed 2.O.R. wounded 11/6/17 following raid by Brigade Village on our left.	AS/.
	11/6/17		Situation normal.	AS/.
	12/6/17		Situation normal.	AS/.
	13/6/17		Situation normal	AS/.
	14/6/17		3 Officers (2/Lt Fox, 2/Lt Whaley & 2/Lt Hill) and 60 O.R. of B Coy were	

WAR DIARY or INTELLIGENCE SUMMARY

Army Form C. 2118.

Place	Date	Hour	Summary of Events and Information	Remarks and references to Appendices
BULLECOURT	14/9/17		A raid on German front line trench between V22c.44.40 and V22c.46.50. Party left our line at 2.15 a.m. - 2 prisoners of 119 R.I.R. captured and a German Machine Gun. The two other German Machine Guns put out of action by bombs. Casualties 2/Lt. E.W. HILLS and 4 O.R. killed. Capt. W. BOWRA, and 2/Lt. G. JOY and 38 O.R. wounded. 7 O.R. missing. Bn relieved in the line by the 2nd Bn Gordon Highlanders & went into camp at MORY. Relief complete 1.20 a.m. on 15/9/17	
MORY	15/9/17		Bn bathing and refitting	
	16/9/17		Bn refitting	
	17/9/17		Bn training & refitting	

Army Form C. 2118.

WAR DIARY
or
INTELLIGENCE SUMMARY.
(Erase heading not required.)

Instructions regarding War Diaries and Intelligence Summaries are contained in F. S. Regs., Part II. and the Staff Manual respectively. Title pages will be prepared in manuscript.

Place	Date	Hour	Summary of Events and Information	Remarks and references to Appendices
MORY	18/6/17		Raw morning	
"	19/6/17		Raw. employed at depth in the lines	
"	10/6/17		Fine evening	N.B.
"	21/6/17		Bn employed at work in the line	N.B.
"	22/6/17		Fine evening	N.B.
"	23/6/17		Bn relieved by 2nd H.A.C. & proceeded to camp at LOGEAST WOOD. 1. O.R. killed. 1. O.R. wounded.	N.B.
LOGEAST WOOD 24/6/17			Fine Evening	N.B.
"	25/6/17		Fine Evening	

WAR DIARY
or
INTELLIGENCE SUMMARY.
(Erase heading not required.)

Army Form C. 2118.

Place	Date	Hour	Summary of Events and Information	Remarks and references to Appendices
LOCRE ST.	26.6.17.		3 Coys entrained for work on Mt HAMEL - THIEPVAL Road. One company entrained evening; L.O.R. occupied	1103
"	27.6.17.			1108
"	28.6.17.		3 Coys. in trenches at HAMEL. One company entrained evening. Coys returned from work at HAMEL. Evening continued	1108
"	29.6.17.		Bn. evening continued	1100
"	30.6.17		Bn. evening continued	1100

R.W. Gordon Major
Comdg. 2/10 Batt. Kings Rgt.

Vol 6

Confidential

War Diary

2/10th Batt. London Regt.

From July 1st 1917
To July 31st 1917

Volume VI

S.C. 128

Army Form C. 2118.

WAR DIARY
or
INTELLIGENCE SUMMARY.
(Erase heading not required.)

Instructions regarding War Diaries and Intelligence Summaries are contained in F. S. Regs., Part II. and the Staff Manual respectively. Title pages will be prepared in manuscript.

Place	Date	Hour	Summary of Events and Information	Remarks and references to Appendices
LOCRE REST	1.7.17.		Bn. being entrained	1226
"	2.7.17.		do	1227
"	3.7.17.		do	1228
"	4.7.17.		do	1229
BRIGADE	5.7.17.		Bn. in support at BRIGADE	1230
TRDGES	6.7.17.		Bn. still in support at TRDGES	1231
"	7.7.17.		Bn. relieved 2 Coys of 1/26th Batt. (170 Rnds to Rt Line) in the Reserve Line at HAPPYCOURT WOOD. Relief completed 1.0 P.M. 2 O.R. Wounded.	1268

T/131. Wt. W708—776. 500000. 4/15. Sir J. C. & S.

Army Form C. 2118.

WAR DIARY
or
INTELLIGENCE SUMMARY.
(Erase heading not required.)

Instructions regarding War Diaries and Intelligence Summaries are contained in F. S. Regs., Part II. and the Staff Manual respectively. Title pages will be prepared in manuscript.

Place	Date	Hour	Summary of Events and Information	Remarks and references to Appendices
HAVRINCOURT WOOD	8.7.17		Situation very quiet. No work for several working parties in the front line	WD
"	9.7.17		Situation very quiet. Working parties found for front line	WD
"	10.7.17		Situation very quiet	WD
"	11.7.17		Situation very quiet. Relieved & billeting of men. Working parties	WD
"	12.7.17		Situation normal. Working parties found for front line	WD
"	13.7.17		Situation normal. Working parties found for front line	WD

WAR DIARY
INTELLIGENCE SUMMARY.
(Erase heading not required.)

Army Form C. 2118.

Place	Date	Hour	Summary of Events and Information	Remarks and references to Appendices
HAVRINCOURT	14.7.17		Situation Normal. Working parties found for front line	WD
WOOD	15.7.17		Situation Normal. Working parties found for the same	WD
"	16.7.17	12.30 P.M.	Situation Normal. B. relieved Hq at 12 a.m. in the front line on the right of the Bde sector. Relief completed 1 O.R. Wounded	WD
"	17.7.17		Situation Normal. Enemy artillery being rather active. Patrols found enemy active. 1 O.R. wounded.	WD
"	18.7.17		Situation normal. Relieved in portion of line by 2/8th B⁵ and moved to portion held by 2/11 B⁶. Relief Completed by 3.30 a.m. Casualties — 1 O.R. wounded accidently. Enemy artillery more active.	WD

Army Form C. 2118.

WAR DIARY
or
INTELLIGENCE SUMMARY.
(Erase heading not required.)

Place	Date	Hour	Summary of Events and Information	Remarks and references to Appendices
HAVRINCOURT WOOD	19/7/17		Situation normal. Enemy artillery a little more active. Casualties 1 O.R. killed 10 O.R. wounded.	J.N.J.
"	20.7.17		Continuous shelling throughout the day, evidently registration. Slackened towards dusk. Raided at 10.30 p.m. See full report attached (a). Total casualties for 24 hours (a) 1 Officer (Capt D. Freeman (unto) wounded. Other ranks 7 killed, 1 died of wounds, 30 wounded.	J.N.J.
"	21.7.17		Situation very quiet. One enemy raider found dead in front of our lines killed by L.G. fire. Enemy artillery fairly silent searching for casualties. Casualties one Officer (2/Lt D.G.G. Walton) wounded no wounded, one killed	J.N.J.
"	22.7.17		Situation quiet. Casualties 2 O.R. wounded	J.N.J.

Army Form C. 2118.

WAR DIARY
or
INTELLIGENCE SUMMARY.
(Erase heading not required.)

Instructions regarding War Diaries and Intelligence Summaries are contained in F. S. Regs., Part II. and the Staff Manual respectively. Title pages will be prepared in manuscript.

Place	Date	Hour	Summary of Events and Information	Remarks and references to Appendices
HAVRINCOURT WOOD	23/7/17		Situation normal. Patrols found enemy active & snipers busy. Casualties One killed.	
	24/7/17		Situation very quiet. Casualties Nil.	
	25/7/17		Situation quiet. Special patrol sent out as per orders attached (1) not successful in obtaining identification. Owing to the fact of a very light by the enemy identical with our signal to withdraw, all that able Officer & 2 scouts withdrew in error. Bombing fight ensued between the latter and four of the enemy in which the Officer (2/Lt Enfield) was wounded & party then withdrew. One of our men was afterwards found (R.J. Young). Casualties 1st 24 hours - One Officer (2/Lt E.S.H. Griffiths) wounded, 6 O.R. wounded 1 missing.	
	26/7/17		Situation very quiet. Relieved in the line by the 9th (2)	

WAR DIARY
or
INTELLIGENCE SUMMARY.

(Erase heading not required.)

Army Form C. 2118.

Place	Date	Hour	Summary of Events and Information	Remarks and references to Appendices
NEUVILLE	27/7/19		Black Watch Relief completed by 12.55 a.m 27/7/19. Casualties 1 O.R. wounded	JJM
			After relief parties Camp at NEUVILLE. Entrained at 5.0 p.m. for BAPAUME. Entrained at BAPAUME and left at 6.0 p.m. for BEAUMETZ arriving 11.0 p.m. proceded by route march to DAINVILLE Casualties Nil	JJM
DAINVILLE	28/7/19		Arrived at DAINVILLE at 1.30 a.m. & occupied billets	JJM
	29.7.19		Battalion training	JJM
	30.7.19		Battalion training	JJM
	31.7.19		Battalion training	JJM

Ch Cowley Cairns Lt Col
Comdg. 2/10th London Regt.

Report of a hostile raid on a sector of the line

held by 2/10th London Regiment.

On the night of 20/21st between 10.30 and 11.30 p.m. the left sector of 175th. Brigade held by the 2/10th. Battalion, The London Regiment, was subjected to a severe artillery bombardment.

Hostile Artillery Barrage Lines.   Barrages were put down on the following lines :

Calibre.	From. To.	Line.
(a) 77.c.m.	10.30 - 10.33.p.m.	Q.3.b.8.7. to K.33.c.5.2.
(b) do.	10.33 - 10.45.p.m.	Q.3.b.7.7. to BUTLERS CROSS
	Fire slackened considerably, ceasing at 11.30.p.m.	
(c) do.	10.45.- 11.30	Q.3.b.7.7. to BUTLERS CROSS.
(d) 8" How.,	10.33 - 10.45.p.m.	Q.3.a.8.10. do. do.
		Drake Street.
	10.45 - 11.30.p.m.	do. do. do.

Fire slackened considerably, ceasing at 11.30.p.m.

(e) 5.9.How	10.33. - 10.45.p.m.	Q.3.A.2.6. to BUTLERS CROSS.
(f) do.	do. do.	Q.3.a.1.5. to Q.3.c.9.50. 8.50.
(g) do.	do. do.	Q.2.d.7.8. to Q.3.c.1.6.
(h) do.	do. do.	Q.3.a.7.10.to Q.3.a.2.6.
(J) do.	10.33. - 11.15.p.m.	Q.3.c.8.4. was kept under fire Battn. H.Q. and R.A.P.

Barrages : (e) (f) (g) (h) (J) . commenced to slacken from 10.45. p.m. until midnight when shelling became very light.

Barrages: (a) and (j) appear to come from the direction of RIBECOURT and GRAINCOURT. The remaining barrages from the other side of TRESCAULT.

MACHINE GUN.   OXFORD VALLEY was swept from 10.33.pm. to 2.0.a.m. with machine gunfire, from the high ground near BOGGARTS HOLE.   SHROPSHIRE SPUR and the ground to the East, was swept from about Q.3.c.5.4. to Q.3.d.5.5.   It was continued intermittently until daybreak.   The fire appeared to come from the direction of DEAN COPSE.

TRENCH MORTARS.   OXFORD VALLEY was shelled from our trenches between

K.33.c.6.1. and Q.3.a.4.2.
K.33.c.6.1. and Q.3.b.4.9.
Q.3.a.1.5Q.6.5Q.and Q3.a.5.4.

The bombardment was intense from 10.30. to 10.45.p.m. and very accurate, the Reserve line, support, old front line, and F sap were badly damaged.
A direct hit was obtained on Battalion H.Q.   Owing to one Coy. Commander being severely wounded during the bombardment, and another Coy. Commander having shown himself totally incompetent to deal with the situation, I ordered the Commanders of the supporting Coy's. to assume command of the troops in the right and left sectors respectively.   Seperate report on this officer is being submitted under seperate cover.   The prompt action of the right front Coy. Commander in at once reinforcing his front line was most commendable, had the officer commanding the left front Coy. acted with similar energy and decision the raiders would not have been able to get a footing in our trenches, and increased damage would have been inflicted.

(2)

S.O.S. call was sent by power buzzer to Battn. H.Qtrs. from the Head of F sap, and right front Coy. H.Q.; in addition it was fired from the front line and Battn. H.Q. The artillery barrage was prompt and effective. Further communication with the artillery was impossible, consequently valuable opportunity of catching the enemy as they withdrew was missed. The artillery communications were unsatisfactory. Wounded were collected at Coy. H.Q. at FACIT DUMP and at a collecting station at the head of TUFNELL AVENUE on the SHROPSHIRE SPUR road. Stretcher bearer squads were sent to these points directly the bombardment slackened, and no difficulty was experienced in getting the wounded to the R.A.P. from where they were at once evacuated. The party from 2/9th Bn. London Regt. arrived in time to be of service in clearing up the situation. The Machine Guns at BUTLERS CROSS, Q.3.a.4.2., Q.2.b.8.7. do not appear to have co-operated as closely as was desirable. It is suggested that a closer liason between O i/c Machine Guns which are placed in Battalion sector, and the Battalion Commander is most necessary. The TRENCH MORTAR which was posted purely for S.O.S. purposes at Q.3.a.7.9. appears not to have fired when the S.O.S. was sent up. It was later knocked out by a direct hit. The above remarks regarding Liason and Battalion Commander it is suggested, could be usefully applied to Trench Mortar Officers. The full power of the defence appears not to be developed due to want of this co-ordination. Casualty report has been rendered under separate cover.

RAIDING PARTY.

Under cover of the barrage a raiding party of strength 100 and 2 officers emerged from HAVRINCOURT PARK at K.33. central, devided into two parties, about 20 to 30, moving on ASHTON ALLEY, along the Western side of the SHROPSHIRE SPUR road ; this party though seen by our patrol which was lying out about K.33.d.9.4. never reached our trenches. The remainder of the patrol advanced in three columns,

(a) <u>The right column</u>, moving across country, on the head of F sap.

(b) <u>The centre column</u>, up OXFORD VALLEY.

(c) <u>The left column</u>, across country on the unoccupied portion of our trench at Q.3.a.7.9.50. This column cut two gaps 5 yards wide in our wire opposite this point.

The right and centre columns, were caught in our Lewis Gun fire from K.33.c.5.1. and never reached our trenches.
The left column, moving down the unoccupied portion of our trench from Q.3.a.7.9.50., obtained a momentary footing in our trench at K.33.c.6.05., but were at once driven out. The raiding party was first seen about 10.35.p.m.
No other attacks materialised. The attack was very feeble, the raiders appear to have lost direction and scattered. There appeared to be no co-operation.

PRISONERS. One wounded man of 86th. K. Fus. Regt. was found in front of our post at Q.3.a.9.9. and brought in. No other wounded men were found.

CASUALTIES. Our casualties all due to hostile barrage were :-

Killed. O.R. 5
Wounded. 1 Officer, 29 O.R.

It is anticipated that the enemy suffered severe casualties from our barrage and Lewis Gun fire.

(3)

GENERAL.   The attack was very feeble and the raiders appeared to have lost their direction. No actual attempt was made to enter our trenches at the head of ASHTON ALLEY, the attacks by the right and centre columns were never actually delivered.
    I wish to bring to notice the excellent work by the following Battalion Runners

422315	Pte Rose G	421461 Pte	Turner W
423372	Tyler W	423352	Johnson J W
423086	James T	422408	Barlow R

All wire communication failed directly the bombardment started. These men continually passed through the barrage and were entirely responsible for keeping me supplied with information as to what was happening.

(sgd) L. D. Sadleir Jackson.

Lieut. Col.,
Commanding 2/10th. Battn.
The London Regiment.

21st. July 1917.

SECRET.   Copy No. _____

                        2/10th. Bn. London Regt.
                        _____

                             PATROL ORDERS.
                             _____

(1) Commander: 2/Lt. Griffiths.

(2) Strength: 1 Sgt. 19 O.R. including 2 Lewis Guns.

3 Object.   (a)   To surprise, destroy or capture occupants
                         of any snipers post encountered, between
                         K.33.d.8.0. and K.33.d.9.2. which will be the
                         extreme limit of action of the patrol.
                         Directly an identification has been obtained
                         the patrol will at once return, the same way
                         as it went out.
                   (b)   To inflict damage by rifle, bayonet, bomb
                         and Lewis Gun fire on the picquet, known to
                         be entrenched from K.33.d.85.10. round
                         Elephant Shelters to K.33.d.90.20. Under no
                         circumstances will any member of the patrol
                         cross to the East of the SHROPSHIRE SPUR road.
                         This picquet will be subjected to a Hurricane
                         bombardment by 2 Stokes Mortars for 2 minutes
                         30 seconds, commencing at 10.30 p.m.

4 Dress: Rifle, blackened bayonet, khaki bandolier
                         round the waist, 2 bombs per man (except Lewis
                         Gunners who will carry revolvers and bombers
                         who will carry a bandolier of bombs, pistols
                         and short daggers.)
                         Steel helmets, faces and hands to be black-
                         ened.
                         1 pair of wire cutters per 2 riflemen per
                         2 bombers, 1pair per Lewis Gun team; (i.e.
                         2 men). Large shears will be carried if possi-
                         ble.

5 Starting   Q.3.b.60.8.5.
   Point.

6 Rallying   Q.3.b.60.8.5.
   Point.

7 Medical   The R.M.O. will arrange for 2 stretcher
   Arrangements.   bearer squads to be at Q.3.b.70.70. (junction
                         of "E" Sap with LANCASHIRE and FUSILIER TRENCH.)
                         Squads to be in possition by 10.30.p.m.

8 ZERO.   Will be at 10.30.p.m.
                         The patrol will leave the starting point
                         at 10.32.p.m.

9 Signals.   The signal to retire will be fired at 11.12
                         p.m. unless the patrol has returned. In any
                         case it will be fired as a directing light
                         for stragglers
                                                          /signal

Contd. (2)

signal 1 green VERY Light fired at 10 seconds intervals for 3 minutes. This signal will be put up on the orders of O/c "C" Company The signal will be fired from a point in DRAKE STREET 50 yards N.W. of BUTLERS CROSS.

Signals False.

Inorder to divert the attention of the enemy from the objective of the patrol; false signals as under will be put up continuously from K.3.b.9.6. O/c "C" Coy. will arrange for these signals to be put up continuously commencing 10.45.p.m. ceasing at 11.10.p.m.
Signals:

(a) 1½" Very lights (White) fired in direction of Q.3.b.8.0. to light up hostile machine guns.

(b) 1" Very lights "Red" fired singly in the same direction.

10 Synchronization of Watches:

Coy. Commanders and patrol leaders will send a watch to Battalion H.Qtrs. at 7. p.m.

11 Trench Mortars:

A Hurricane barrage by the Stokes Mortar Battery will be fired on the objective commencing 10.30.p.m. The garrison will occupy FUSILIER TRENCH during this bombardment. The patrol LANCASHIRE TRENCH.

12 Listening Posts.

Will be withdrawn at 10.25.p.m. and put out again at 11.15.p.m.

13 Artillery.

An 18 pdr barrage will be put down on the S.and W. outskirts of MOW COPSE from K.33.d.4.41 to K.33.d.7.2. and from K.33.d.7.2. to K.33.d.8.5. This barrage will commence at 10.32.p.m. and will be continued until 11.p.m.

14 Machine Guns:

A box barrage will be formed from K.33.d. 4.4. to K.33.d.7.4. from K.33.d.7.4. to K.33.d.95. 20.(through the N. edge of N. elephant shelter). The Machine Guns forming this barrage will fire from Q.2.b.8.7. and Q.4.d.4.8.. Another Machine Gun will fire on K.33.d.9.5. 20. from Q.4.d.4.8. These machine guns will maintain an intense barrage between 10.32.p.m. and 11.p.m. gradually slackening fire after 11.p.m. ceasing at 11.30 p.m. A German Machine Gun will be fired down SHROPSHIRE SPUR road skirting the West side of the road. Position Q.3.b.7.7. This gun will maintain an intense fire up to 11.15.p.m. when it will cease, but remain in position. A block to limit the traverse West of the Western edge of the"SHROPSHIRE SPUR road" will be "fixed".

15 Secondary Patrols.

A diversion will be made commencing at XXXXXXXXX 10.25.p.m. by O.C. "A" Coy. against

/ the first

Contd.   (3)

the first hostile barricade in OXFORD VALLEY, situated at Q.3.c.9.7., and rifle pits to W. This will take the form of a bombardment by rifle grenadiers pushed forward on both sides of OXFORD VALLEY for a distance of 70 yards, machine gun enfilade fire on OXFORD VALLEY up to and including BOGGARTS HOLE. Lewis Gun fire on K.33.c.4.2. from guns in the outpost line of left sector. Enfilade Lewis Gun fire along our wire, searching dead ground in front of Left front platoon Right front Coy. from Q.3.a.8.9.70. This diversion will be continued up to 11.15.p.m. when it will gradually die down, ceasing at 11.30.p.m. The listening posts in front of Right and Left sectors will be withdrawn so as to be in our outpost line by 10.20.p.m. They will be put out again at 11.15.p.m.

No Very lights or signals will be fired. Intense bursts of fire will be maintained during the period 10.25.pm. to 11.15.p.m.

Rifle grenadiers will continually change there position laterally.

16 **Intelligence and Hostile Wire.**   The Battalion Scouts will put out a tape and cut a gap 3 yards wide through the German wire at Q.3.b.70.95. The patrol tape will be joined to this tape at the German wire.

(Sgd) L.W.Sadleir-Jackson,Lt. Col
Commanding 2/10th Battalion,
The London Regiment.

25.7.1917.

Army Form C. 2118.

WAR DIARY
or
INTELLIGENCE SUMMARY.
(Erase heading not required.)

Vol 7

CONFIDENTIAL

WAR DIARY

of

2/10th Bn London Regt.

from 1st Aug. 1914 - 31st Aug. 1914

(VOLUME 7)

WAR DIARY
or
INTELLIGENCE SUMMARY.
(Erase heading not required.)

Place	Date	Hour	Summary of Events and Information	Remarks and references to Appendices
DAINVILLE	1/8/17		Battalion training	
	24/8/17		Left Dainville & to entrained at Arras for Proven	
	25/8/17		Detrained at Proven & proceeded to Sixty Bucks being near Q Vlamertinghe.	
	26/8/17		Preparations were for going into action	
	27/8/17		do	
	28/8/17		headed to Canal Bank Camp & went into Bivouac there.	
	29/8/17		Went into the line at St Julien, relieved the 1/5th Gloucesters & the 1/4th Royal Berks. Casualties { 8 wounded 2 missing	
	30/8/17		Situation normal Casualties { 1 O.R. wounded 1 missing	
	31/8/17		Situation normal Casualties { 1 O.R. wounded 1 missing During this tour of the line we received 5 O.R. of the following formations 2 of 1/5 Gloucesters 3/ Oct 1/8 Hussars 1 of 1/9 R.E. 4 June 5 M.G.C. 1 unknown Battalion	

Radclyffe Parker Lt Col
Commanding 2/10th Hampton Regt

Army Form C. 2118.

175/58

Vol 8

WAR DIARY
or
INTELLIGENCE SUMMARY.

Confidential
War Diary of
2/10th London Regt.

from 1st September 1917 — 30th September 1917

(Volume 8)

Army Form C. 2118.

WAR DIARY
or
INTELLIGENCE SUMMARY.
(Erase heading not required.)

Instructions regarding War Diaries and Intelligence Summaries are contained in F.S. Regs., Part II. and the Staff Manual respectively. Title pages will be prepared in manuscript.

Place	Date	Hour	Summary of Events and Information	Remarks and references to Appendices
St Julien	31/8/17 to 1/9/17		Relieved in Front Line by 2/11 Bn London Regiment. Relief completed by 2.0 am	
	1/9/17		Casualties 6 OR killed (including 1 OR reported missing on 30/8/17) 20 OR wounded + 2 wounded at duty remaining at duty	a
	2/9/17		Battalion took over billets on CANAL BANK	
	2/9/17		Battalion moved from CANAL BANK (which was taken over by 29 Bn London Regt) to DAMBRE CAMP	a
	2/9/17 to 14/9/17		Battalion training. 5 OR wounded 1 OR at duty by enemy MG which was firing at our OPs on 4/9/17. 1 OR attached to Brigade HQ wounded on 4th inst. 2 ORs accidentally wounded on 11/9/17.	a
	11/9/17		Battalion marched into "C" Hutments BRAKE CAMP	a
	12/9/17		Reported that Lieut R.O.Rees attached to 176th Brigade HQs as Intelligence Officer gassed and 1 OR wounded also attacked.	a
	12/9/17		Battalion rested.	
	13/9/17 to 16/9/17		Time devoted to cleaning up and refitting of equipment. Battalion training. During this period the 6 Battalion enabled to a working party of 3 Companies to hand. Such on nights 16/9/17 Sept. Casualties nil	aaa
	16/9/17		Battalion moved to REIGERSBURG CAMP.	

WAR DIARY or INTELLIGENCE SUMMARY

Army Form C. 2118.

Place	Date	Hour	Summary of Events and Information	Remarks and references to Appendices
	20/9/17		Battalion moved into huts on the Canal Bank.	a.
	20/9/17		Attack on [...] Relieved 2/5th & 2/6th Batn London Regt on line at Mon Du Hibou — Poelcappelle Sector on night of 21/22nd Sept 1917. Relief carried out though counter attack barrage. Arrived in time to be of material assistance to troops in the front line in repelling attack. 2/Lieut C.E. Dunlop killed 21/22-9-17. 4 Bars & N.C.O.s & 12 ORs wounded.	a.
	22/9/17		Heavy shelling throughout the day. Enemy seen massing at Aviatik Farm dispersed by our Artillery. Supply tank destroyed by E.A. at Wanbertinghe at 10.30am. Casualties 21/22/9/17. 3 ORs killed 12 ORs wounded 4 ORs killed 10 ORs wounded.	a.
	23/9/17		Enemy troops seen on front subject lively area shelling between Queeea and Strop Farm. Attack beaten off by counter attack in evening. Artillery Casualties 22-23/9/17. 5 ORs killed 22 ORs wounded. 2/Lt J.G. Smiley wounded since died on 24/9/17.	a.
	24/9/17		Heavy area shelling all day. Relieved at night the 2/4 London Regt & 2 Cambria at St Julien: 2 Londonia at California Drive Battn H.Qs at Cheddar Villa & Juliet Farm. In addition of 2/9 & 2/12 London London Regt. Casualties 23-24/9/17. 3 ORs killed 15 ORs wounded.	a.

WAR DIARY or INTELLIGENCE SUMMARY

Army Form C. 2118.

Place	Date	Hour	Summary of Events and Information	Remarks and references to Appendices
	25/9/17		Enemy Aeroplanes bombed CALIFORNIA DRIVE causing the following casualties:- 2 ORs killed, 15 ORs wounded. Shell fired early from Rear Headquarters struck by heavy shell. Casualties:- 2 ORs killed, 1 OR wounded (2 remaining on duty). Night quiet. Other casualties:- 4 ORs killed, 22 ORs wounded. The 2/4th and 2/12 Bn. London Regiment attacked at 5-50 AM.	a
	26/9/17		Our Companies from ST JULIEN moved up as reinforcements to the front line at noon. Our Companies from CALIFORNIA DRIVE moved to ST JULIEN. Baker HQ at HACKNEY VILLA. Intense barrage on ST JULIEN – WINNIPEG ROAD – CLUSTER HOUSES. CASUALTIES 25-26/9/17:- 2/Lieut R.R. Biddle killed. 8 ORs wounded. 5 gassed.	a
	27/9/17		Morning not quiet. Our Companies from ST JULIEN relieved and moved back to CANAL BANK and hence to DAMBRE CAMP. Two Companies from front line were relieved and marched DAMBRE CAMP at 4 ROAM on 28 Sept. 17. CASUALTIES 26-27/9/17:- 6 ORs wounded.	a
	28/9/17		In Camp. Hostile Aeroplanes bombed vicinity of Camp at night. Casualties nil.	a
	29/9/17		In Camp. Hostile Aeroplanes bombed Camp area at night. Casualties nil.	a a
	30/9/17		Battalion moved from DAMBRE CAMP to BRAKE CAMP "O" Hutments at noon.	a

Army Form C. 2118.

WAR DIARY
or
INTELLIGENCE—SUMMARY.
(Erase heading not required.)

Confidential

War Diary
of
2/10th Battn London Regiment

From 1st October 1917 — 31st October 1917

(Volume 9)

Army Form C. 2118.

WAR DIARY
or
INTELLIGENCE SUMMARY.
(Erase heading not required.)

Place	Date	Hour	Summary of Events and Information	Remarks and references to Appendices
	1/10/17		Battalion moved from "C" Hutments BRONZE CAMP to XVIII Corps area to NEUELES LES ARDRES in RECEPER area under the administration of XIII Corps	JS
	2/10/17		Battalion arrived at 7 A.M. and took over new billets at NIELLES LES ARDRES. The remainder of the day troops busied expired attention being paid to clothing & equipment.	JS
	3/10/17		Training in accordance with training syllabus. 30 yards range started. Town Majors Orders re pre-cautionary measures against fire, etc., issued to all companies and notices placed in all billets	JS
	4/10/17		Training in accordance programme	JS
	5/10/17		"	JS
	6/10/17		"	JS
	7/10/17		"	JS
	8/10/17		Battalion carried out Musketry practice on V Army 'B' Range	JS
	9/10/17		Training in accordance programme	JS
	10/10/17		Brigade Tactical Scheme carried out on V Army "B" Area. After balais to ooo	JS
	11/10/17		Training in accordance with programme. Afternoon Battalion falled in was issued with chocolates	JS
	12/10/17		"	JS
	13/10/17		Live Gun firing on RECQUES field firing range	JS
	14/10/17		"	JS

WAR DIARY
or
INTELLIGENCE SUMMARY.

(Erase heading not required.)

Army Form C. 2118.

Place	Date	Hour	Summary of Events and Information	Remarks and references to Appendices
Nieppe	15/10/17		Training in accordance Programme. Reconnaissance & drill Conference of all Brigade officers re coming operations.	
	16/10/17		Training in accordance Programme. Ceremonial drill Inspection of 1st Line Transport	
	17/10/17		Presentation of Medals by G.O.C Division at NIEPPE.	
	18/10/17		Training. Practice attack with Battalion Area.	
	19/10/17		" " " by Battalion in 3rd Army B. area.	
	20/10/17		Battn entrained at Caestre and detrained at Gare Poperinghe & thence marched to Road Camp. Before the Bergen XVIII Corps Area.	
Houtte Ryn	21/10/17		Training in accordance with Programme	
	22/10/17		Attack Practice on Ground over to preliminary operations near Poelcappelle.	
	23/10/17		Brigade Practice attack do	
			Battle began Personnel left for Road depot halted at Houthulst after Inspection by Brigadier General H.R. Cuthbert D.S.O.	
	24/10/17		Battalion Baths	
	25/10/17		Reconnaissance of ground for Battn attack carried out by C.O. & Company Commanders & report of Line Transport officer & Prototype officer.	

Army Form C. 2118.

WAR DIARY
or
INTELLIGENCE SUMMARY.
(Erase heading not required.)

Instructions regarding War Diaries and Intelligence Summaries are contained in F.S. Regs., Part II. and the Staff Manual respectively. Title pages will be prepared in manuscript.

Places	Date	Hour	Summary of Events and Information	Remarks and references to Appendices
Montau Brayer	26/10/17		Platoon training under remainder of 9 Coys	Q
	26/10/17		Company and Platoon training in accordance with programme and	Q
	27/10/17		Preparation for to-nights summary of operation	Q
	28/10/17		do	Q
	29/10/17		do	Q
	30		Battalion moved to Dury Camp near Vianchy.	Q
	31st		Battalion moved to Coupel Rouch	

Referring, Major 1/10 B London Regt
Commanding 1/10 B London Regt

Army Form C. 2118.

Vol 10

WAR DIARY
or
INTELLIGENCE SUMMARY.
(Erase heading not required.)

Instructions regarding War Diaries and Intelligence Summaries are contained in F. S. Regs., Part II. and the Staff Manual respectively. Title pages will be prepared in manuscript.

Confidential
War Diary
2/10th Battalion London Regiment

From 1st November 1917 — 30th November 1917
(Volume 9)

Place	Date	Hour	Summary of Events and Information	Remarks and references to Appendices

WAR DIARY or INTELLIGENCE SUMMARY

Army Form C. 2118.

Place	Date	Hour	Summary of Events and Information	Remarks and references to Appendices
Hooge Canal Bk	1/4/17		Battalion bathed and preparations made for going into the line	Q
	2/4/17		C & D Coys moved forward to Kruispoom Park	Q
	3/4/17		Batt. Headquarters and A & B Coys moved forward to Kruispoom Park. Working parties detailed by Bay Commdg. of Brigade to carry out R.E. work to Ghelen farm. Parties about 150 supplied for A B C & D groups 5/8 till 8 o'clock next day.	Q
	4/4/17		Above reconnoitred. We found line from Hellas Trench to Towers Farm. The above working parties again provided.	3 Q
	5/4/17 6/4/17		Large Wire entanglement commenced went & working parties furnished. Relieved 7/11 Yorkshire Reg in the line Battalion front. Hellas Towers on the left to Lewes Tower on the right in front of Philisofelle. Relief very difficult owing to much Bomshin and shelf Shelter & 6" Howtier fire. No men returned as killed & wounded not got away from the Railway front.	Q Q Q
	7/4/17		A Patrol under 2/Lt Henderson & Pte Rankin & 19 OR Cpl Butler scouts to front & out towards Splen & Ronda to attain identification from the enemy. 22 Ronda were taken & over 20 killed besides some wounded. Our casualties 2 OR slightly wounded. Known to have happened but there let our men get back.	Q

WAR DIARY
or
INTELLIGENCE SUMMARY.
(Erase heading not required.)

Army Form C. 2118.

Place	Date	Hour	Summary of Events and Information	Remarks and references to Appendices
In the line	7/4/17		6 our line rested portion from	C
	8/4/17		Battalion relieved by 2/4th the London Regt in the line & moved back to	C
			Regl Camp near Montenescourt.	C
Regl Camp	9/4/17		Rest and cleaning of clothes & equipment.	C
	10/4/17		Battery Battery Chart Party the Patrols under 2/Lt C.F. Henderson	C
			which captured 25 hostile prisoners inspected by Major General A.B.E.	C
			Cayley D.S.O. Commanding 88th Division and congratulated on their gallantry &	C
			Sunday. Voluntary Church Parade and cleaning of Camp.	C
	11/4/17		Training under Company arrangements.	C
	12/4/17		Training under Company arrangements. Draft and	C
	13/4/17		Bombers of Battalion fired on Range.	C
	14/4/17		Battalion moved to PRIVETT CAMP - PRONEN.	C
Privett Camp	15/4/17		Training under Company arrangements. Battle surplus rejoined.	C
	16/4/17		Training under Company arrangements and Company Drill	C
	17/4/17		Platoon training under Company Commanders supervision.	C
	18/4/17		Church Parade & Recreation.	C

WAR DIARY
or
INTELLIGENCE SUMMARY.
(Erase heading not required.)

Army Form C. 2118.

Place	Date	Hour	Summary of Events and Information	Remarks and references to Appendices
Proven Camp.	19/10/17		Inspection of Camp by Major General A.B.E. Cator. Camp SE Ayr. Battalion went through baths	
	20/10/17		Training in vicinity of Camp. Inspection of Box Respirators by Divisional Gas Officer.	
	21/10/17		Inspection of Baths by Commanding Officer. Company training during the day. Advance party for Lumbres area left by lorry	
	22/10/17		Training under Company arrangements.	
	23/10/17		Training under Company arrangements. A Proven Platoon formed under 2nd in Command to be a separate unit. H.W.+ Mess separate.	
	24/10/17		Training under Company arrangements. Recreation	
	25/10/17		Church Parade. Recreation	
	26/10/17		Transport moved by road to ST. MOMELIN to billet there night of 26/27". Companies carried on training in vicinity of Camp.	
	27/10/17		Battalion moves to BAYENCHEM — (Lumbres area). by rail from PROVEN to WIZERNES — Transport moved from ST MOMELIN to BAYENCHEM.	

WAR DIARY
or
INTELLIGENCE SUMMARY.
(Erase heading not required.)

Army Form C. 2118.

Place	Date	Hour	Summary of Events and Information	Remarks and references to Appendices
	28/4/17		Inspection of new area. C.O. Batt. to attend conference of Bde. Bn. & Coy. C.O.'s. Capt Lyons took command of Battalion	
	29/4/17		Firing on Range by A Coy. Other Companies carried on training under Company Commanders	
	30/4/17		Firing by B & C Coys. (D Coy Butt Party) Remainder carried out Platoon training and organisation	

4/1/17

M.J.Fortescue Lieut Colonel
Comdg 7th London Regt

WAR DIARY or INTELLIGENCE SUMMARY

CONFIDENTIAL.

WAR DIARY

of

2/10 Bn. LONDON REGT.

from 1st December 1917 to 31st December 1917.

(Volume II.)

WAR DIARY
or
INTELLIGENCE SUMMARY.

Army Form C. 2118.

Place	Date	Hour	Summary of Events and Information	Remarks and references to Appendices
Bayenghem (LUMBRES) (area)	1/12/17		"Bn. Hd. Corps" used Range. — "A" Coy Bn. but Parts. — Remainder carried out Platoon training. Reorganisation of Coy, returned from Conference.	Q
	2/12/17 – 3/12/17		Voluntary Church Service. Recreation. Battalion went through Baths. Coys when not bathing carried out training in vicinity of billets.	Q
	4/12/17		Coys carried or training area during morning. Snipers and Scouts paraded for Special training. Battalion paraded in evening for night operations.	Q
	5/12/17		Platoon training under supervision of Company Commanders in billeting area. Transport moved from BAYENGHEM to ST. MOMELIN en route to SIEGE CAMP (by road)	Q
	6/12/17		Battalion (less Transport) moved from BAYENGHEM to SIEGE CAMP Entrained at WIZERNES detrained at ELVERDINGHE. Transport moved from ST. MOMELIN to ST. TANTER BIEZEN.	Q
SIEGE CAMP ELVERDINGHE	7/12/17		Transport completed journey by road moving from ST. TANTER BIEZEN to SIEGE CAMP. The C.O., Company Commanders, Signals and	Q

WAR DIARY or INTELLIGENCE SUMMARY

Army Form C. 2118.

Place	Date	Hour	Summary of Events and Information	Remarks and references to Appendices
Poelcapelle Sector	8/2/17		Intelligence officers reconnoitred the sector of the line to be taken over by this Battalion. Platoon training carried out and preparation made for the line. Special preventive treatment against trench feet applied to all feet.	
			Battalion went into line in support, relieving 4 Glos Coy. Three Companies in EAGLE TRENCH one in CANDLE TRENCH Battalion HQ at DOUBLE COTS. Casualties nil.	
	9/2/17		Battalion in support – Same dispositions as on 8/2/17. Casualties nil.	
	10/2/17		Battalion relieved 2/m Londons in front line. Sec. Lee killed on 3 Company front. Casualties 1 OR Killed 4 OR wounded.	
			Situation normal and fairly quiet.	
	11/2/17		Situation normal & everything quiet. Some shelling of tracks. Casualties Nil.	
	12/2/17		Inter Platoon relief of all fronts in front line. Situation normal. Some shelling of tracks. Casualties 1 OR Killed 2 OR died of wounds. 4 OR wounded. 1 OR wounded at duty.	

WAR DIARY
or
INTELLIGENCE SUMMARY.
(Erase heading not required.)

Army Form C. 2118.

Place	Date	Hour	Summary of Events and Information	Remarks and references to Appendices
Polygonbeke Sector.	13/9/17		Situation quiet. No action on either side. Casualties 4 O.R. wounded (including 3 gas cases)	
	14/9/17		Situation normal. Battalion in front-line relieved by 7th Gordons. Battalion moved back into supports in EAGLE TRENCH and CANDLE TRENCH. Casualties 2 O.R. wounded	
	15/9/17		Batts in support. Casualties - 3 wounded O.R. 1 O.R. wounded at duty.	
	16/9/17		Batt. relieved by 7th Gordons and marched to billets on CANAL BANK. Battalion in close Divisional Reserve. During tour in line 10/14th Decr. all ranks were wet duckboarded, drained and were provided with shelter. Many feet received treatment	
CANAL BANK	17/9/17		Cleaning and rest in CANAL BANK Billets. Men's feet attended to and men receiving foot rubbing sent to foot rubbing stations for preventive treatment against trench feet.	
	18/9/17		Light training under company commanders. Baths were attended by Battalion	

WAR DIARY
or
INTELLIGENCE SUMMARY

Army Form C. 2118.

(Erase heading not required.)

Place	Date	Hour	Summary of Events and Information	Remarks and references to Appendices
Canal Bank	19/10/17		GOC Brigade addressed all officers & Platoon Sergeants in Church Army Hut SEGI CAMP. Platoon training carried out during morning under NCOs left in camp. Working parties & stretcher parties supplied for work in YPRES under Town Major.	Q
	20/10/17		Platoon training. Similar working parties supplied to Town Major YPRES as on 19/10/17.	Q
	21/10/17		Platoon training with Company Commanders. Working hard for coming Major YPRES supplies as on 19th & 20th.	Q
	22/10/17		Platoon training. Company Commanders reconnoitred the sector of the line to be taken over on 24th. Owners of B Battery the chat. Notified.	Q
	23/10/17		Filling & equipping the line. Special attention paid to precautions against Trench feet. Church Parade Divine in afternoon in commemoration of all of the Battalion who had fallen.	Q
	24/10/17		Battalion relieved 2/4 London in the line.	Q

WAR DIARY
or
INTELLIGENCE SUMMARY
(Erase heading not required.)

Instructions regarding War Diaries and Intelligence Summaries are contained in F. S. Regs., Part II. and the Staff Manual respectively. Title Pages will be prepared in manuscript.

Army Form C. 2118.

Place	Date	Hour	Summary of Events and Information	Remarks and references to Appendices
In the Line Poelcappelle & Langemarck Sector.	24/12/17		Dispositions in the line as follows. From Left to Right. D Coy Tank Farm & Berthen House. C Coy Senegal Farm, Besace Farm & Wake Farm, Bower Houses. "B" Coy Jordan House. Stray Houses, Compromise Fm & 2 posts at Reguete Farm. Relief carried out successfully & without casualties. The Coy HQ were as follows. D Coy Tank Farm. C Coy Senegal Farm, "B" Coy Jordan Hse. A Coy was in close support or counter attack positions & were situated at Olga Houses Coy HQ. The posts for this Coy were:- Millers Hses, Lapegrie Fm, Kangaroo Huts & Lemnos House.	[illegible]
	25/12/17		Christmas Day. A quiet day on the whole, there was intermittent shelling. No casualties. Snow fell & covered the whole battlefield, hiding tracks etc.	[illegible]
	26/12/17		Situation quiet on the front but Artillery on both sides very active. Enemy planes flew very low over Jordan House driven off by Lewis gun fire. Casualties 3 O/R wounded.	[illegible]
	27/12/17		Front posts heavily shelled, some short shooting by our Artillery on Senegal. Casualties 4 O/R wounded.	[illegible]
	28/12/17		Situation quiet on front line. Battn HQ at Louis Farm very heavily shelled. Eagle Dump hit, several boxes & Very Light ammunition blown up. Enemy aeroplanes very active one dropped lights on Millers Houses. Casualties Capt. R. Pattison commanding D Coy killed by a shell, 2 O/R killed 5 O/R wounded. Battalion relieved in the front line by 2/10th London Regt. Battalion moved back to position in supports as follows:- A. B & D Coys in Eagle Trench. C Coy HQ at [illegible]. Capt G. Hall "C" Coy in charge. Battn HQ moved to Pig & Whistle	This should be entered under date 27/12/17 [illegible]

2449 Wt. W14957/M90 750,000 1/16 J.B.C. & A. Forms/C.2118/12.

WAR DIARY
or
INTELLIGENCE SUMMARY

(Erase heading not required.)

Army Form C. 2118.

Instructions regarding War Diaries and Intelligence Summaries are contained in F. S. Regs., Part II. and the Staff Manual respectively. Title Pages will be prepared in manuscript.

Place	Date	Hour	Summary of Events and Information	Remarks and references to Appendices
In the Line Poelcappelle & Langemarck Sector.	28/12/17 contd		in Langemarck. D Coy moved back to Candle Trench. Battn now in Support Left Sector. Capt. & Adjt. T. Gould, Capt. G. Hall, Capt. K.S. Bowron, Capt. I. Gluckstein mentioned in Despatches. Congratulatory telegram from Brigadier.	
	29/12/17		Coys in Eagle Trench set to work putting up Barbed Wire defences & building & improving dug-out accommodation & fire positions. S.O.S. sent up by the Division on our left & barrage put down on enemy lines, this died down after an hour and the situation became normal again. Commanding Officer & the Adjutant dined with Brigadier.	
	30/12/17		Thaw begins to set in. Situation quiet during the day. Our artillery put down barrage along the front of Division on our left & on our front & then concentrated about Turenne Crossing & Colibri Farm, a Raiding party of two Coys left Vache Farm at 8.0 pm in order to capture & hold the above places.	
	31/12/17		Quiet day. Carrying parties provided to carry rations & ammunition to 2/11 Bn in the line. About 11.0 pm Germans sent up series of coloured lights all along the front. Evidently a New Year celebration.	

R. W. Gotthorp
Lt Col.
Commanding 2/10 Bn London Regt.

2449 Wt. W14957/M90 750,000 1/16 J.B.C. & A. Forms/C.2118/12.

War Diary

of Eton Lines Depot

from 1st January 1918
to 31st January 1918

Volume I

Army Form C. 2118.

WAR DIARY
or
INTELLIGENCE SUMMARY

(Erase heading not required.)

Instructions regarding War Diaries and Intelligence Summaries are contained in F. S. Regs., Part II. and the Staff Manual respectively. Title Pages will be prepared in manuscript.

Place	Date	Hour	Summary of Events and Information	Remarks and references to Appendices
In the line Inquench	1-1-18		Battalion in support was relieved by 2/4 Londons and moved out to billets on CANAL BANK.	
Canal Bank	2.1.18		Battalion went through baths. Cleaning of equipment etc and inspections.	
"	3.1.18		Platoon training under Company Commanders. Working party of 1 officer and 50 O.Ranks provided for shovelling trick rubble at YPRES.	
"	4.1.18		Battalion celebrated Xmas. Holiday Xmas Dinner.	
"	5.1.18		The whole Battalion worked on the Army Defence system. Work carried on from 7.15 am to 3 pm.	
"	6.1.18		Whole Battalion worked on the Army Defence system. Same as on 4/1/18.	
"	7.1.18		Battn. moved from CANAL BANK to HERZEELE and occupied billets.	
Herzeele	8.1.18		On account of extreme Cold men were kept on the move by sharp marches, drill etc	
"	9.1.18		Marching Close Order drill and manual. Heavy falls of snow and acute cold.	
"	10.1.18		Brigade Parade to rehearse an inspection by Corps Commander at a little later date.	

WAR DIARY
or
INTELLIGENCE SUMMARY

(Erase heading not required.)

Army Form C. 2118.

Instructions regarding War Diaries and Intelligence Summaries are contained in F. S. Regs., Part II. and the Staff Manual respectively. Title Pages will be prepared in manuscript.

Place	Date	Hour	Summary of Events and Information	Remarks and references to Appendices
Tergeele	11-1-18		Platoon training and Vigorous service on account of cold weather prevailing.	GWB
"	12.1.18		Battalion Parades attended Corps Commanders Inspection at HOUTKERQUE Road. Presented by Corps Commander, to Officer & other Ranks who has not previously been decorated with distinction won.	GWB
"	13.1.18		Church Parade. Memorial Service for Capt R. Rattray Pollin who has fallen in action.	GWB
"	14.1.18		Musketry practice on Ranges A.M. in afternoon C.O. Corps in morning N.C.O's of No's 1 & A+B Coys under R.S.M. for instruction in morning N.C.O's of C+D in afternoon.	GWB
"	15.1.18		Route March – HOUTKERQUE – WATOU – DRAGLANDTE – WINNEZEELE	GWB
"	16.1.18		Company training under Company Commanders.	GWB
"	17.1.18		Platoon training under Company Commanders.	GWB
"	18.1.18		Platoon training under Company Commanders.	GWB
"	19.1.18		Platoon training under Company Commanders.	GWB

Army Form C. 2118.

WAR DIARY
or
INTELLIGENCE SUMMARY

(Erase heading not required.)

Instructions regarding War Diaries and Intelligence Summaries are contained in F. S. Regs., Part II. and the Staff Manual respectively. Title Pages will be prepared in manuscript.

Place	Date	Hour	Summary of Events and Information	Remarks and references to Appendices
Herzeele	20.1.18		Battalion entrained at PROVEN (after light railway from HERZEELE) for move by rail to VILLERS BRETONNEAUX.	G/B
Villers-Bretonneaux	21.1.18		Battalion detrained at VILLERS BRETONNEAUX Station and marched to billets in FOUILLOY.	G/B
FOUILLOY	22.1.18		Coy. parties at disposal of Company Commanders for labour and Company training. Corporals under special signal instruction. Battalion parade for CO's inspection in afternoon.	G/B
	23.1.18		Batt. Lewis Gunners carried out Musketry on Range. Lewis Gunners remained in billeting area for Lewis Gun training. Sports in afternoon.	G/B
	24.1.19		Tactical route march & artillery formation practice.	G/B
	25.1.18		Musketry on Range and practice in deployment.	G/B
	26.1.18		Coy parties at disposal of Company Commanders. Inspection of Box Respirators by Brigade Gas Officer. Baths allotted to Batt. in afternoon.	G/B
	27.1.18		Church Parade. Sports.	G/B
	28.1.18		Platoon and Coy training in Morning. Sports in evening. Specialist training 1hour in evening.	G/B

Army Form C. 2118.

WAR DIARY
or
INTELLIGENCE SUMMARY

(Erase heading not required.)

Instructions regarding War Diaries and Intelligence Summaries are contained in F. S. Regs., Part II. and the Staff Manual respectively. Title Pages will be prepared in manuscript.

Place	Date	Hour	Summary of Events and Information	Remarks and references to Appendices
Souilly	29.1.18		Musketry on Range. Lewis Gunners carried out Lewis gun training in billeting area. Cross country run sports in afternoon.	
	30.1.18		Battalion on training area for a tactical exercise. Lewis Gunners carried out Lewis gun training in billeting area.	
	31.1.18		Battalion proceeded to training area for outpost scheme. Lewis Gunners in billeting area, carried out Lewis Gun training	

R. Westerham
Lieut. Col.
Comdg. 1/10 London Regt.

Army Form C. 2118.

WAR DIARY
or
INTELLIGENCE SUMMARY

(Erase heading not required.)

Instructions regarding War Diaries and Intelligence Summaries are contained in F.S. Regs., Part II. and the Staff Manual respectively. Title Pages will be prepared in manuscript.

Place	Date 1918	Hour	Summary of Events and Information	Remarks and references to Appendices
FOUILLOY	Feb 1st		Training under Company Commanders in Musketry, Platoon and Company drill. L.Gunners on range.	
	2nd		Battalion training in tactical exercise on training area.	
	3rd		Church Parade, Brigade Transport Competition at which this Unit won first prize.	
	4th		Companies under Company Commanders for deployment drill, musketry, Close Order drill & gas drill.	
	5th		Companies paraded under Company Commanders, Equipment inspected and fitted properly. Sports in afternoon.	
BOIS DE VEVILLE.	6th		Battalion moved. Entraining at CORBIE, detraining at APILLY. then ce moved by bus to billets in BOIS DE VIEVILLE. Became the left supporting battalion of Brigade in the line.	
	7th		Relieved 2nd Wilts Regt in the line at VENDEUIL, three Companies in front line, one Company in reserve in VENDEUIL FORT. Battn.H.Q. in VENDEUIL FORT. Casualties Nil.	
Line.	8th		Situation in sector quiet. Casualties Nil.	
	9th		Situation remained quiet. Considerable individual movement observed in the enemy's lines. About 50 shells fell in this sector during the day. Day and night patrols sent out to reconnoitre ground in OISE VALLEY. Casualties Nil.	
	10th		Enemy still quiet. The usual movements observed in the enemy lines. Nil Casualties.	
	11th		Situation quiet. A few shells on VENDEUIL FORT and VILLAGE. Individual movement observed in the enemy lines to a large extent. Patrols sent out at night all along the front. The river and canal in NO MAN'S LAND make patrolling difficult. Casualties Nil.	
	12th		Situation still quiet. No enemy activity beyond the usual individual movement Casualties Nil	
	13th		Situation still quiet. The usual observed movemnts in the enemy lines. Casualties Nil. Patrols sent out at night to reconnoitre.	

Army Form C. 2118.

WAR DIARY
or
INTELLIGENCE SUMMARY

(Erase heading not required.)

* Instructions regarding War Diaries and Intelligence Summaries are contained in F. S. Regs., Part II. and the Staff Manual respectively. Title Pages will be prepared in manuscript.

Place	Date	Hour	Summary of Events and Information	Remarks and references to Appendices
LINE	Feby 14		Situation unchanged. Little activity on enemy's part. Usual movement observed. Casualties Nil Patrols sent out all along this unit's front at night.	
	15th		Quiet day. Slight shelling of VENDEUIL FORT and VILLAGE. Considerable individual movement observed in enemy lines, and sounds of hammering and work in progress heard. Casualties Nil. Usual patrols out at night.	
	16th		Situation remained quiet. H A. increasingly active over our lines. Our artillery appear to be more in evidence. Considerable movement seen in enemy lines and sounds of work heard day and night. Casualties Nil. Patrols went out at night as usual.	
	17th		Little activity on either side. Patrols out at night but difficult to get in frequent and close touch with enemy to ascertain their dispositions and alertness on account of river, canal, and marshes. Casualties Nil.	
	18th		Situation quiet. Casualties Nil. Patrols out in NO MAN'S LAND during night. Casualties Nil.	
	19th		Situation quiet during day. At night patrol crossed canal and reconnoitred but were strongly attached by the Boches. A sharp encounter took place. Five of enemy were shot down by Lewis Gun, our casualties 1 killed two wounded (O.R.) During evening about 7 p.m. enemy bombarded VENDEUIL FORT with small H.E. Casualties 2 O.R. wounded. Total Casualties 1 O.R. killed, 4 O.R. wounded	
	20th		Quiet day. Slight artillery activity on both sides. Patrol out at night. Casualties.	
	21st		Situation quiet and unchanged. Usual individual movement observed. Casualties Nil	
	22nd		Quiet during day. Relieved at night by 12th London Regiment, and moved into camp at VIEVILLE WOOD. Casualties Nil.	
BOIS DE VIEVILLE	23rd		Cleaning of equipment and clothing etc. Battalion in is Left Support Battalion for Defence of Battle Zone. Battalion put through baths,	

Army Form C. 2118.

WAR DIARY
or
INTELLIGENCE SUMMARY

(Erase heading not required.)

Instructions regarding War Diaries and Intelligence Summaries are contained in F. S. Regs., Part II. and the Staff Manual respectively. Title Pages will be prepared in manuscript.

Place	Date 1918	Hour	Summary of Events and Information	Remarks and references to Appendices
BOIS DE VIEVILLE	Feb 24.		Working on Battle Zone defences.	
	25th.		Battalion relieved in the BOIS de VIEVILLE by 8th. East Surreys, and proceeded to AUTREVILLE and PIERREMAND, near CHAUNY.	
	26th.		Reconnaisance of new Battle Zone at BUTTES de ROUY by Commanding Officer, Adjutant and Company Commanders.	
	27th.		Headquarters, "A" Coy. & "D" Coy. moved to positions at BUTTES de ROUY. Battalion Headquarters and "A" Coy in dug-outs and huts at BUTTES de ROUY and "D" Coy. in Sunken Road. "B" Coy. and "C" Coy. moved to billets in SINCENY.	
	28th.		"C" Coy. moved into dug-outs at BUTTES de ROUY. Alarm given, all Companies stood to ready to man Battle positions. "B" Coy. (Counter-attack Coy). moved from SINCENY to BUTTES de ROUY Battalion under 15 minutes notice.	

Lieut.-Colonel,
Commanding, 2/10th. Battalion, The London Regiment.

WO 14

175/58

[War Diary]
2/10" London Regt
Volume III
March 1st - 31st
1918.

Army Form C. 2118.

WAR DIARY
or
INTELLIGENCE SUMMARY.
(Erase heading not required.)

Instructions regarding War Diaries and Intelligence Summaries are contained in F. S. Regs., Part II. and the Staff Manual respectively. Title pages will be prepared in manuscript.

Place	Date	Hour	Summary of Events and Information	Remarks and references to Appendices
Butte de Warl.	Mar 1		Working parties on positions in the Battle Zone.	
	2		Working parties on positions in the Battle Zone.	
	3		Working parties on positions in the Battle Zone.	
	4		Working parties on positions in the Battle Zone.	
	5		Working parties on positions in the Battle Zone.	
	6		Working parties on positions in the Battle Zone.	
	7		Working parties on positions in the Battle Zone. Commander in Chief visited area & inspected positions.	
	8		Outpost line reconnoitred by Company Platoon Commanders.	
	9		Working parties on positions in the Battle Zone.	
Sus.	10		Relieved 9th Londons in Outpost Line. Battalion H.Q. in AMIENY ROY. Casualties nil.	
	11		Situation quiet. Capt. R. Holt and 1 guide of 9 Londons went out to reconnoitre No Mans Land. Capt. Holt missing, guide returned wounded. On afternoon Batt. H.Q. was heavily shelled.	

WAR DIARY
or
INTELLIGENCE SUMMARY.
(Erase heading not required.)

Army Form C. 2118.

Instructions regarding War Diaries and Intelligence Summaries are contained in F. S. Regs., Part II. and the Staff Manual respectively. Title pages will be prepared in manuscript.

Place	Date	Hour	Summary of Events and Information	Remarks and references to Appendices
Line	March 12th		Situation quiet except for slight shelling of village of AMIGNY ROUY. Strong patrol of 40 O.R. under Capt Rpt Chapman went out at night. Enemy were encountered. Casualties 2 O.R. killed, 3 O.R. wounded.	
	13th		Situation quiet. Casualties nil. One Boche Prisoner captured near our lines.	
	14th		Situation quiet. Night patrols working on No Mans Land. Casualties 1 O.R. died of wounds	
	15th		Situation quiet. Usual night patrolling of No Mans Land. Casualties nil.	
	16th		Situation quiet. Casualties Nil.	
	17th		Situation quiet. Casualties Nil.	
	18th		Relieved in out post line by 9th Gordons. Battn H.Q. moved back to BUTTES DE ROUY. Casualties Nil.	
	19th		Work on the Battle Zone Defences. Casualties Nil.	

WAR DIARY or INTELLIGENCE SUMMARY

Army Form C. 2118.

Place	Date	Hour	Summary of Events and Information	Remarks and references to Appendices
Line	Mar. 20		Work on Battalion Defences - Counter Mt. Batt. received orders from Higher Command to "prepare for attack." No unusual action taken.	
	21st	4.30 am	At 4.30 am heavy bombardment opened on our sector in vicinity of BUTTES DE ROY and the west front-line was not shelled to any extent. Very heavy gunfire heard to the North in direction of St Quentin. Observation was impossible owing to dense fog which rested on the ground larger part of the day. Bombardment eased somewhat about 4 pm but shelling was kept up throughout the night. No attack developed on our sector. Battle positions were manned at onset of the bombardment. 1 OR killed & wounded.	
	22nd		Shelling of our Support positions continued with MG fire. Considerable shelling of our Support position & village of AMIGNY ROUY. Fog prevailed in morning but visibility was poor throughout the day. Short snipits continued to the North and existence of German advance seen in the shape of German OP's aloft to the rear of our original line. Very heavy fighting in progress at CONDREN visible from our OP. 1 OR killed 3 wounded	
	23rd		Our front-line at AMIGNY ROUY was shelled fairly heavily intermittent. Shelling of BUTTES DE ROUY and road from BUTTES to VINCENT very heavy fighting evidently in progress to our North. Large number German OP's seen to the North well behind our original line. Enemy probably penetrated our positions to a considerable depth. 1 OR died of wounds & 4 wounded	

WAR DIARY
or
INTELLIGENCE SUMMARY.
(Erase heading not required.)

Army Form C. 2118.

Place	Date	Summary of Events and Information	Remarks and references to Appendices
	Mar. 24th	No actions developed on our sector. Forward positions gas shelled + rear positions shelled with HE. Heavy fighting seen to our North. 3 O.R. wounded.	
	25th	Hostile Artillery on our sector quiet. Enemy transport troops to be seen advancing on roads to our North. Casualties Nil.	
	26th	Situation quiet on Bn Sector. Bn. relieved by 1/7th London Regt. 2 Companies moved to SINCENY. 2 Companies to AUTREVILLE. Batn. HQ. at AUTREVILLE.	
	27th	Batn. HQ. moved to PIERREMAND. Casualties 2 O.R. killed 1 O.R.W. wounded by E.A. during night.	Wagon lines shelled with 4.2's PIERREMAND shelled
	28th	Situation quiet. Casualties Nil.	
	29th	Situation in Support quiet. Casualties Nil.	

Army Form C. 2118.

WAR DIARY
or
INTELLIGENCE SUMMARY.
(Erase heading not required.)

Place	Date	Hour	Summary of Events and Information	Remarks and references to Appendices
Porchingues	March 30		Bn relieves 9th Londons in line. Casualties Nil.	
	31st		BUTTES DE RON shelled. Direct hit on O.P. Casualties 1 o.r. Killed. Situation otherwise All quiet.	

S Bazin
Major
2nd in Comd. Lt.Col.
Comdg. 7/10 London Regt.

175th Inf.Bde.
58th Div.

2/10th BATTN. THE LONDON REGIMENT.

A P R I L

1 9 1 8

War Diary

9/10 Jordans

Volume II

April 1918

Army Form C. 2118.

WAR DIARY
or
INTELLIGENCE SUMMARY.
(Erase heading not required.)

Place	Date	Hour	Summary of Events and Information	Remarks and references to Appendices
Bois de Rouy	1		Situation quiet. Intermittent shelling during day. 2 Coy relieved by 1 Unit (263 R.I.F) Casualties 1 Other Rank sent out as G.P.S.	
	2		Enemy raided W.P. post. Captured gun & 1 man. Slight shelling during day. Relief by 263rd R.I.F. completed. Preparations to previous trenches & billets. Casualties –	
	3		Camp shelled heavily in afternoon with heavy guns. Casualties 2 O.R. killed. In evening Battn marched to Le Mesnil and billeted in caves.	
Le Mesnil	4		Battn moved by march route to LAVERSINE and went into billets.	
	5		Battn marched to LONGPONT. Entrained at LONGEAU.	
Longeau	6		Detrained in morning at LONGEAU and marched to GENTELLES WOOD. No shelling of wood. Casualties Nil.	
Gentelles	7		Moved to bank behind VILLERS BRETONNEUX. Situation quiet.	
Bretonneux	8		Slight shelling of position with gas.	
	9		Enemy shelling at rear of position. Relieved 9th London Regt. in VILLERS BRETONNEUX. Counter attack in progress at time of relief on both flanks of enemy. Nothing encountered.	

Army Form C. 2118.

WAR DIARY
or
INTELLIGENCE SUMMARY.
(Erase heading not required.)

Place	Date	Hour	Summary of Events and Information	Remarks and references to Appendices
Green Trenches	April 10		Situation unchanged. Continued shelling. N.E. of gas.	
	11.		Situation unchanged. The usual heavy shelling but oft & gas.	
	12.			
	13th		Relieved McKenzies at Bois l'ABBE. Slight shelling.	
	14th			
	15th		Slight shelling of forward Companies & batteries at rear.	
	16. } 17th		Moved to BLANGY TRONVILLE. Occupied trenches Hills. Slight shelling in vicinity of village. Rested in BLANGY TRONVILLE.	
	18.		Marched to GENTELLES. Heavy shelling of Cavalry.	
	19.		Village shelled throughout the day. & slight shelling of Company providing outposts the village.	
	20.		Relieved by 1st Londons and moved to Sunken road W.M.A.	
	21.		Slight shelling of position. Light barrage put down at dusk by British & Kent.	
	22nd		Light enemy shelling. Light barrage put down by British & Kent at dusk. 2nd Lieut. V Kent at dusk severe. Cas: 1 Her wounded (since died of wounds) 1 Lieut. Lt Dunham wounded	

A5834 Wt.W4973/M637 750,000 8/16 D. D. & L. Ltd. Form/C.2118/13.

WAR DIARY or INTELLIGENCE SUMMARY

Army Form C. 2118.

(Erase heading not required.)

Place	Date	Hour	Summary of Events and Information	Remarks and references to Appendices
Haucourt Sector	1916 24th		After desultory bombardment the enemy put down at 4.0 am enemy attacked on Haucourt Sector at 6.0 am. This Bn was counter attack Batt. to 173 Bde. Batts. were immediately found up as its counter attack positions. At 7.30 am a report was received that left Bn of 173 Brigade front line had been compelled to yield ground. One Company was dispatched to form a defensive flank. Before another Counter attack the Co. Lieut Col W.P. Symonds DSO personally reconnoitered towards Haucourt and he was shot by a sniper. Body returned & evacuated. Capt. T. Tower(adjt) took command of the Battalion. Orders were given for Counter attack at 10.30 am. First attack was held up by heavy M.G. fire from Haucourt Wood and was had to dig in after losing 200 yards. Three companies were ordered to reinforce 173 Bde front line. At 5 pm. Londons took over our dispositions as Counter attack Batt. At night elements of the Bn were held in reserve to 9th London & Sig. Pas. who counterattacked a big gap formed in our line on right of 9th London & Coy to help were sent up filled this gap. N.I.O.&. Morlie wounded	
	25th		Disposition of previous night maintained Bn relieved on night of 25/26 @ a.a. by 12th Londons Co. dug in r.e.s. 9th Londons & trops of units of 174 Brigade	
	26th		Moves by road route to PONT DE METZ occupied billets	
	27th		Moves by march route to LE MESGE & occupied billets	
	28		Marched to AILLY LE HAUT CLOCHER occupied billets	
	29 30		Rested.	

Lowell Captain
Comdg 7/6 London Regt.

Army Form C. 2118.

175/58

WAR DIARY
or
INTELLIGENCE SUMMARY.
(Erase heading not required.)

War Diary
2/10th London Regt

Volume V
May 1918.

Army Form C. 2118.

WAR DIARY
or
INTELLIGENCE SUMMARY.
(Erase heading not required.)

Instructions regarding War Diaries and Intelligence Summaries are contained in F. S. Regs., Part II. and the Staff Manual respectively. Title pages will be prepared in manuscript.

Place	Date	Hour	Summary of Events and Information	Remarks and references to Appendices
LINE	MAY 16th		Relieved 18 Gordons in left sub-sector of Brigade front known as "The Fairfair".	
	17th		Situation quiet. Casualties Nil	
FRONT LINE	18th		About 200 shells on Batt. sector during day. Barrage put down by our artillery on enemy front and support line. Enemy artillery replied in response to 2 red lights sent up from his front line. Enemy M.G.s active during night. Casualties 2 O.R. wounded.	See annexed Summary
	19th		Situation normal. Slight shelling over the sector. Enemy M.G. active sweeping over front line posts. Casualties 1 O.R. killed 5 O.R. wounded	
	20th		About 150 shells on Batt. during day. Situation otherwise quiet. Registration carried out by enemy artillery on front line. Casualties 5 O.R. wounded	
	21st		No change. Usual shelling of Batt. sector. Some movement seen in enemy's trenches. Hostile aircraft kept up a continuous patrol over our line during early hours of the morning. Casualties Nil	
	22nd		Hostile artillery slightly less active. 16 T.M. shells on front line. On night of 22nd Batt. was relieved by 2nd Gordons and moved back to vicinity behind HENENCOURT WOOD	
HENENCOURT WOOD	23rd		Rest & cleaning up. Casualties Nil.	
	24th		Light training in vicinity of billets.	

Army Form C. 2118.

WAR DIARY
or
INTELLIGENCE SUMMARY.
(Erase heading not required.)

Instructions regarding War Diaries and Intelligence Summaries are contained in F. S. Regs., Part II. and the Staff Manual respectively. Title pages will be prepared in manuscript.

Place	Date	Hour	Summary of Events and Information	Remarks and references to Appendices
HENENCOURT WOOD	25th		Training in vicinity of billets.	
	26th		Church Parade in morning. Bombing Competition in afternoon.	
	27th		Rifle training in morning. Lewisbry competition in afternoon. On night 27/28. Bn relieved 6th London in HENENCOURT VILLAGE and MELBOURNE TRENCH. Batt/HQ and 2 Coys in former - 2 Coys in latter. Casualties NIL. (Batts went into support in MILLENCOURT SECTOR)	
	28th 6 31st		In Support in MILLENCOURT SECTOR. (see attached Summary of events.) Casualties 28th 1 OR Killed 1 wounded 29th Nil 30th 1 OR wounded 31st Nil	

Mawler
Lieut Col Comdg
7th London Regt

WAR DIARY
or
INTELLIGENCE SUMMARY.
(Erase heading not required.)

Army Form C. 2118.

Place	Date	Hour	Summary of Events and Information	Remarks and references to Appendices
~~VILLERS~~ AILLY LE HAUT CLOCHER	1-5-18		Resting — Cleaning up & inspections	
	2nd		Rest —	
	3rd		Training — Gas drill — close order drill — N. Sports in afternoon	
	4th		Musketry. Battalion fired practices on range at FAMECHON in morning. Sports in afternoon.	
	5th		Memorial Service to the late Lt.Col. W.F.T. SYMONDS. D.S.O. and all others of the unit who fell in recent fighting. Transport moved by road to find staging area at BOURDON. Battle surplus attached and sent to III Corps R.C. at VILLERS SOUS AILLY.	
	6th		Battn. moved by bus to MOLLIENS-AUX-BOIS and after debussing marched to BAZIEUX, occupying billets. Transport arrived at final destination BOIS ROBERT near BAZIEUX.	
BAZIEUX	7th		Battalion moved into reserve trenches in front of BAZIEUX.	
	8th		Bn. in reserve. — Work on BAZIEUX defences. Casualties 2 O.R. wounded	
LINE	9th 10 15th		Bn. in reserve. Work on BAZIEUX defences. Casualties Nil. (9/5/18 Major E.P. Lawson appointed to command Bn. Capt F. Gould 2nd in command).	

War Diary.

THE HAIRPIN - ALBERT.

On the evening of 16th May the Battalion relieved the London Irish in a sector known as The Hairpin, N.W. of ALBERT.

Officers.

Headquarters.
    Lt.Col. E.P.Cawston.   Commanding.
    Capt.   V.A.Finlayson.   Adjutant.
    2/Lieut. R.W.Chamberlin.   Signals.

'A' Company.
    Major S.Bowers, Lieuts. C.W.Ardley, I.H.Sly, and Idris.

'B' Company.
    Captain E.A.Bye, Lieuts. A.V.Stout, & R.G.Edwards.

'C' Company.
    Lieuts. Burton, Le Breton, Clarke.

'D' Company.
    Lieuts. Berrell, Smetham, Struebig.

Attached maps show the dispositions -

'A' Right Forward.   'B' Left Forward.
'C' Support.   'D' Reserve.

The Quartermaster (Capt. Armishaw) and Transport Officer (Capt. Jackson) remained at Battalion Transport Lines in the BOIS ROBERT South West of BAIZIEUX.
On the right were the 9th Londons. On our left the 17th Royal Welsh Fusiliers and *later* the 15th Cheshires.

The feature of the period in the line was the very definite nature of the information sent to us from higher authorities almost daily that the enemy were expected to attack on the ALBERT - ARRAS Front. Prisoners captured in various parts of the line were apparently convinced that these were the enemy's plans and actual dates were passed down to units. With the exception of the fact that our patrols found the enemy active in the trenches N.E. and S.E. of The Hairpin salient, nothing unusual occurred.
On the night of the 18th one platoon of 'C' Company in support was sent up to thicken 'B' Company's sector Left Forward.
The Hairpin had been *raided* by Storm Troops about a fortnight before we took over, and retaken. The trenches in the salient were battered about and shallow. We buried 25 German bodies.
On the evening of the 20th an inter-Company relief took place leaving
'D' Coy. Right Forward.
'C' "   Left Forward.
'B' "   Support.
'A' "   Reserve.

One platoon of 'B' remained Left Forward but was withdrawn before the Battalion was relieved on the night of 22nd by 3rd Londons (173rd Inf.Bde) under Lt.Col.Sandars.
During the early hours of the relief the enemy gassed fairly heavily the valley about W.19.central, which was the route for relief and where limbers met outgoing Companies, but no casualties were sustained.

Casualties during the period in the Hairpin Salient - 1 killed, 12 wounded.

The Battalion on relief proceeded to bivouacs in HENENCOURT WOOD.

Attached panarama shows a view of the Hairpin Salient as seen from the spur occupied by 9th Londons on our right.

Attached are patrol orders, and relief orders.

2/10th London Regiment.

Issued to O.C. 'A', 'B', 'C' Companies.

PATROL ORDERS.

Two Reconnaissance Patrols will be sent out tonight at midnight mainly with the object of finding out the position of advanced German posts with a view to scuppering them tomorrow night.

Although the patrols are mainly reconnaissance, they must understand that in the event of their having an opportunity of obtaining an identification tonight, they must do so tonight.

'A' Coy. will send a patrol towards W.21.d.central.
'B' " will send a patrol towards W.21.b.8.8.

All identifications are to be removed from the patrol, e.g. letters, badges, identity discs and paybooks. Raiders' discs will be issued by O's.C.Companies. Sergeant Shaw will report to O.C. 'A' Company at 9 and to O.C.'B' Company at 10 p.m. tonight.

Each patrol will consist of one officer and 7 men selected by him.

Dress: Rifle, bandolier, (soft cap or tin hat at patrol leader's option) 2 bombs per man, but the rifle and bayonet are the essential weapons.

On return of patrol O.C. Company will report "GURKA".

E.P.CAWSTON.
Lt.Col.

18/5/18.

P.S. Patrol leader to send in rough written report at "stand to" and to report to Battalion H.Q. with one of his patrol at 7-0 a.m.

Password :- GHURKA.
All screens to be warned.
Battalion H.Q. will notify Battalions on left and right.
O's.C. 'A' & 'B' will notify Companies on left and right.

2/10th London Regiment.

PATROL ORDERS.

'C' and 'D' Companies will send patrols out at 11 p.m. in the direction of W.21.b.8.3. and W.21.d.2.8.respectively.

Each patrol will consist of 1 Officer and 5 O.R. and will push sufficiently far forward to be warned of any special enemy movement or assembly and will remain out until just before dawn.

Patrol leaders will obtain full information of recent patrols from Lieuts. STOUT and SLY respectively.

If either patrol leader is satisfied that the enemy is assembling, he will send word back to his Company Commander "BOIL RIGHT" or "BOIL LEFT" according as it is the right or left Company that reports.

On receipt of this message from patrols, O.C.Company will (i) inform Battn.H.Q. by runner and by wire,
(ii) inform the other forward Company Commander who will inform his patrol and both patrols will remain out with a view to obtaining confirmatory evidence.
(iii) inform support and reserve Companies who will at once "Stand To".
(iv) order his Company to "Stand to". Before artillery fire is asked for Battn.H.Q. will order both patrols to be withdrawn.

Identifications are urgently required and both patrols must do their best to secure one if occasion arises. Each patrol leader will carry a Very pistol and 6 rounds and must realise that unless he is certain that the movement he sees is an assembly he must not report "BOIL".

Usual precautions regarding reid,discs, badges, letters &c

Soft caps or steel helmets at patrol leader's discretion.

Password "RATIONS".

Codeword to report Patrol is withdrawn "RATIONS RIGHT" or "RATIONS LEFT".

E. P. CAWSTON.
LT.Col.
Comdg.2/10th Londons.

20/5/18

2/10th London Regiment.

Relief Orders. Evening 22nd May 1918.

1. The 3rd Londons will relieve 10th Londons in left Sector of the Brigade front this evening.

2.   'A' Coy. of 3rd relieving 'A' of 10th
    'B' " " " " " 'B' " "
    'C' " " " " " 'C' " "
    'D' " " " " " 'D' " "

Relieving Companies will arrive in that order.

3. Guides at rate of 1 per platoon and 1 per Company H.Q. will rendezvous at Battn.H.Q. at 8-30 p.m. and report to Lieut.Greenwood at Battn.H.Q. These guides <u>must come down by trench</u> and leave their Company H.Q. at the following times.
    'A' Company at 5 p.m.
    'B'   6 p.m.
    'C'   7 p.m.
    'D'   8 p.m.

4. With regard to 'A' Company ;-

'A' Coy. of 3rd Londons will enter the Company Sector at W.20.d.9.7. and immediately upon entering at this point 'A' Coy. of 10th Londons will file out at W.20.b.6.1. and proceed by track.

With regard to 'B' Company;- as soon as each platoon is relieved the Company will assemble in the deep communication trench between LGA BRIDGE W.21.a.3.4. and W.20.b.9.1. and when assembled will file out by the track. O.C.'B' will order good steps to be cut at W.20.b.9.1. to facilitate egress.

With regard to 'C' Company, as soon as 'C' Company of 3rd Londons arrives, 'C' Coy. of 10th will close up to its left and leave by the Communication trench running down between our sector and the Cheshires, as soon as the whole relieving Company is in the trench.

With regard to 'D' Company;- 'D' Coy. of 3rd Londons will enter the Company Sector at W.21.a.7.4 and as soon as the whole Company is in, the two left platoons will file out to their left and the two right platoons will file out by W.21.c.5.8. i.e. their right. The Company will assemble in the deep communication trench between W.21.a.3.4. and W.20.b.9.1. and move out from there as soon as O.C.'D' Coy. has them assembled.

5. Each Company of 'C' and 'D' Companies will leave 4 men on sentry duty until midnight at which hour these men will proceed to Battn.H.Q. to report to R.S.M.3rd Londons and Lce/Cpl Smith of 10th Londons Intelligence Section.

6. Companies on relief will proceed to cross roads at V.22.c.8.8.where guides and Coy.Qmr.Sgts.will meet them and guide to bivouacs in HENENCOURT WOOD.

7. Distance between platoons 100 yards.

8. Relief to be conducted in silence.

9. L.G.limbers will be at Aid Post at 10 p.m. Guns,Pouches and stretchers will be loaded there and limber will follow each Company.

Each Company will send 1 Lewis Gun N.C.O. to the Aid Post at 9-45 p.m.

The R.S.M. will detail N.C.O. to see that these limbers are drawn up in order 'A', 'B', 'C', 'D', facing West with 10 yards between each limber.

10. Company Mess boxes will be sent to Battn.H.Q. with 2 orderlies per Company fully equipped at 9-45 p.m. These orderlies will proceed with the Mess Cart.

11. All tools will be deposited at each Company Headqrs. before 8-30 p.m. tonight O's.C.Companies will see that none are left lying about. All pickets and wire will be dumped in dumps chosen by Company Commanders in front line.

12. All handingover certificates will be carefully prepared receipts being made out on one certificate for S.A.A., Grenades, Hand and R., Picks, Shovels, etc. etc., Trench Maps and aero-photos.

13. All food containers and petrol tins will be delivered to Battn.H.Q.by the guides detailed in para 3, supplemented if necessary.

14. On completion of relief each Company Commander will send an officer to report the fact to Battalion Headquarters. Companies will not wait for this officer to return.

15. Battalion Headquarters will, on relief, open at V.26.a.5.9.

E. P. CAWSTON.
Lieut. Colonel.
Comdg.2/10th Londons.

22/5/18.
1-30 p.m.

2/10th London Regiment.

MILLENCOURT SECTOR.

On the night of 27th May the Brigade relieved the 174th Brigade in the MILLENCOURT Sector ; the 9th Q.V.R. taking over the right forward sub-sector, the 12th Rangers, taking over the left forward sub-sector, and the 2/10th relieving the 6th Londons in support.

The bivouacs in HENENCOURT WOOD vacated by the 2/10th were taken over by the 7th Londons.

The following officers went forward with the Battalion :-

    Lieut.Colonel E.F.Cawston.
    Capt. V.A.Finlayson. Adjutant.
    Lieut.Stout I.O. and L.G.O.
    Lieut.Chamberlin, Signals.

'A' Coy.
    Major S.Bowers. Lieuts. Idris and Greenwood.

'B' Coy.
    Capt. Davis, Lieuts.Edwards, Martin, Sturton.

'C' Coy.
    Lieut.Cranmore, Aris, Clark, Parker.

'D' Coy.
    Capt.Berrell, Lieuts.Struebig and Tuffley.

The Stores (Capt.Arnishaw) and Transport (Capt.Jackson) remained in BOIS ROBERT S.W. of BAIZIEUX.

H.Q., 'A' & 'B' Companies were disposed in cellars in HENENCOURT with battle positions in WALLASY TRENCH. 'C' & 'D' Companies were in MELBOURNE TRENCH SOUTH. 'D' on the right in touch with the 9th Q.V.R., 'C' on the left in touch with 12th Rangers.

Attached "handing over statement" and maps as handed over to the 8th East Surreys(55th Bde 18th Divsn) who relieved the Battalion on the night of 31st May/1st June shows the dispositions.

The dug-out intended for advanced Battalion Headquarters was not completed by relief. Skeleton of two platoon of 'A' Company were on the night of relief sent forward to occupy a line of old shelters in V.29.a. so that the relieving Battalion might take these over.

It had been intended that the Brigade were to stay in the line until the night June 2nd/3rd, in which event the 2/10th Bn were to have relieved the 9th Q.V.R. in the line but the relief by the 55th Brigade was put forward to the night of May 31st/1stJune.

During the night 30/31st our M.G.'s. and artillery carried out vigorous harassing fire on the enemy's possible assembly positions W. of ALBERT and gas was discharged. This brought about retaliation in the form of H.E. and Gas on HENENCOURT and MILLENCOURT from about midnight to 3 a.m.

Attached is copy of a map captured from a prisoner in another sector showing the proposed method by which the enemy intended to capture MILLENCOURT and HENENCOURT.

On the night of 31st/1st the Bn. was relieved by 8th East Surreys under Lieut.Colonel Irwin D.S.O. During the relief (which was completed about 12.45 a.m.) the situation was particularly quiet although the gunners and T.M.'s on our left were conducting at intervals a bombardment preliminary to an attack by the 55th Division on AVELUY WOOD. The Battalion had tea at the Transport Lines (BOIS ROBERT) and moved to bivouac camp near BEHENCOURT arriving in Camp about 3-45 a.m. on June 1st.

Casualties during the period in the line were 1 O.R.killed and 2 wounded.

Midnight 27/28 May.

S.P.104.

To
Headquarters
175th Infantry Brigade.

I.   I have given orders to my two Companies in KANSNCOURT that in the event of KANSNCOURT being heavily shelled or gassed they are to move forward into COURT TRENCH and be disposed, one Company on the North of main road and up to V.28 central One company on the South and down to D.4.b.7.3.

II.   In the event of your giving me orders "ATTACK- MOVE" these two Companies will move ; one to WALLABY TRENCH from V.30.a.5.3. to junction with WATTLE STREET and make and be prepared to man fire bays in WATTLE STREET facing N.; and one in WALLABY TRENCH from V.30.c.5.6. to V.30.a.5.3. and make and be prepared to man fire steps in the communication trench from V.30.c.8.8. to V.30.a.5.9.
       This to resist any attack from the North.

III.   Paras. I. and II are pending your contrary order and in absence of defence scheme handed over.

May 27/28.

E. P. CAWSTON.
Lieut.Colonel.

Headquarters.   S.F.106
175th Infantry Brigade.

In view of the enormous amount of work required in and about the trenches occupied by our forward Companies and in WALLABY, and that the wire near WALLABY is not on the side of the trench from which according to captured maps attack is most likely to come, may we hand over to L.T.M.B. or other unit the Gas Guard at Brigade, Guard over S.A.A. at Brigade,Guard over wells in HEBUTERNE,Loading party at W.D.Dump HEBUTERNE - Total: 4 N.C.O's and 22 men

II. Our right forward Company whose trenches are in bad condition and whose wire is weak and shelters few, has to find 12 men to haul sandbags out of a dug-out which is being made for M-G. May I point out that there are a dozen M-G.teams in the locality who do little or no work.

III. With regard to the position of my two forward Coys. it is obvious that the valley is untenable without possession of the spurs on either side. It is also I assume extremely probable that any hostile operations would include gassing the valley in which event the position of the garrison of my right forward Company would be untenable. I am also confident that as the valley in front of my right forward Company is quite flat, that portion could, if

reasonably wired, be made impassable to the enemy by L.G. fire from either flank; the L.G.posts being protected by the terraces and slightly higher than the low lying ground.
I should be glad if I might move half my right forward Company from the valley and place it in the trench running up the slope about E.1.c.3.4.to E.7.a.2.9. In this position it would form a useful switch line in event of the garrison of Southern spur being driven in and it would at the same time control its portion of the valley and - in daylight - influence the Northern spur. Its present position at any rate is unsound.

IV The same remarks apply to an extent and in principle to the position of my left forward Company and I consider that it would be more usefully placed if half were disposed in AUSTRALIA TRENCH from its junction with MELBOURNE to VALLEY TRENCH. There is now a certain amount of useful and vacant accommodation in AUSTRALIA and fire bays facing across the valley. It will be necessary to make a few fire bays in the terrace N. of AUSTRALIA as at present the occupants of AUSTRALIA would be at the mercy of the enemy on the Northern spur in the same way as they are now.

V. I would suggest similar work in AUSTRALIA W. of the junction with MELBOURNE.

VI. A certain amount of fire can be brought to bear on the Northern spur from the rear of the present positions of my forward Companies and with your approval I propose putting up wire on what is now our sky line, i.e. from V.30.b central to W.25 a.central.

VII During my reconnaissance of the forward area we shall be taking over on 31st/1st, I noted
(a) The junction of trenches about W.26.c.central lends itself to being made a strong point.
(b) The traverses of the communication trench running back from E.2.a.central are exceptionally puny and the trench when filled in by a few near shells would be enfiladable by rifle fire and useless.

VIII   Having studied the routes from HENENCOURT to WALLABY I feel that we should lose 25% of our support Companies when moving up from HENENCOURT. I should prefer if you are agreeable, that these Companies occupy and work on the trenches they are to garrison and a lot of time would be saved going to and fro.

IX   Good Company or Battalion Headquarters are ready for occupation on the reverse slope at V.29.a.central and the dotted line shown in N.W.corner of that square. May we take over tonight please ?

E.P.CAWSTON.
Lt.Col.
Commanding 2/10 th Londons.

28/5/18
1-30 p.m.

Headquarters S.P.112.
　175th Infantry Brigade.

I. 　　Reference Support Battalion Headquarters, I enquired last night of the Tunnellers, and am informed
(i) that there is no telephone wiring to the dug-out.
(ii) The dug-out will not be ready before Saturday. Its use for H.Q. at present is out of the question. It could be used in emergency by half a dozen men. I draw your attention again to V.29.a.7.5. as suitable for personnel of Battalion Headquarters at once. The unfinished dug-out would accommodate C.O. and observers. It is obvious that my H.Q. could not remain in HELLNCOURT and I should be glad to have permission to take over V.29.a.7.5. as advanced H.Q. at once so that I may inform my Company Commanders.

II. 　　Please say where Brigade Advanced Relay Post will be in the event of my receiving orders to move forward.

III. 　　May I have a reply to or approval of contents of my S.P.102 of 27/28th and paras. I and II of my S.P.106 of 28th.

　　　　　　　　　　　　　　　　　E.P.CROUCH.
　　　　　　　　　　　　　　　　　　Lt.Col.
29/5/18.　　　　　　　　　　　Commanding 2/10th Londons.

B.P.115.

To all Companies.   SECRET.

2/10th Londons.

I.   Reference B.P.114, this Battalion will not relieve the 9th Londons in the line but <u>will be relieved</u> by a Battalion of 55th Brigade, the 8th East Surreys.

II.   On relief the Battalion proceeds to bivouacs about 4,000 yards S.W. of BAILLEUX.

III.   Officers of relieving unit will reconnoitre to-day or to-morrow. Each Company must have an officer ready to and able to show them their dispositions when they arrive.

IV.   After work tonight all tools of 'C' & 'D' Coys. are to be dumped at point where track cuts MELBOURNE in V.30.d.9.4. approx. where limber will be.

V.   O's.C.Coys. will bear in mind that all tools delivered to them form Battalion Mobile Reserve and unless tools to the number of delivered are returned tonight, they will be paid for.

	Picks.	Axes.	Shovels.	Saws.	Bill-hooks.
'C'	35	-	40	-	5
'D'	35	2	37	-	5
'B'	20				

VI.   O's.C. 'A' & 'B' Coys. will return to R.E. Dump before 10.0 a.m. tomorrow morning all tools obtained from R.E.Dump and will send receipts to Battalion Headquarters forthwith.

VIII.   'A' & 'B' will endeavour to give all L.Gunners practice with L.G.firing during to-day and to-morrow on improvised ranges in the village.

                                    B.P.CAMPION.
                                    Lt.Col.
                                    Commanding 2/10th London Regt.

30/5/18
11 a.m.

'A','B','C','D'
Q.M. and T.O.

S.P.121.

RELIEF ORDER.

I. The Battalion will be relieved tomorrow evening by 8th East Surreys 55th Brigade.

II. Company Commanders of relieving unit have reconnoitred.

III. 'D' East Surreys will relieve 'A'
'A' " " " " " 'B'
'C' " " " " " 'C'
'B' " " " " " 'D'

IV. Guides, one per platoon and two per Coy.H.Q. will report to Lieut.Stout at Battalion Headquarters at 9-30 p.m. Under arrangements to be made by him they will at 10-30 p.m. meet 8th East Surreys at V.27.c.9.5. Incoming companies will arrive at rendezvous in order 'B' 'C' 'A' 'D'.

V. All trench and disposition maps and trench stores and S.A.A. will be handed over and receipts obtained.

VI. Each Company will on relief send an officer to Bn. H.Q. to report.

VII. Companies on relief will proceed by route V.28.c.4.4. - D.4.a .30.95. - D.4.a.5.t. - D.5.b.4.2. and across track not shown on map to V.27.c.5.5. Thence to BATTALION H.Q. where guides will meet them and take them to position near Transport Lines where they will have tea and then proceed to bivouacs about U.20.b and C.21.a.

VIII. Advance parties of 5 per Company will report to Q.M. at Transport Lines by noon tomorrow. Q.M. will arrange for advance parties to report to representative of Staff Captain at junction road and track at C.22.a.7.5. at 4 p.m. tomorrow and for guides for Companies to the camps allotted to them.

IX. Breakfasts will be issued on arrival in camp.

X. There will be no movement of formed bodies of troops East of HENENCOURT before 9-30 p.m. West of this line distances of 200 yards will be maintained between Companies.

XI. Transport Lines and Q.M.Stores will not move.

XII. On completion of relief Brigade H.Q. will open at BAVELINCOURT C.7.c.2.8.

XIII. On arrival in camp Companies will report the fact to Battalion Headquarters.

XIV. Pioneers will proceed to camps to arrange necessary latrines, tables, notice boards, etc., before arrival of battalion.

XV. Canteen will be open before arrival of Battalion.

XVI. Officers' chargers will be at Bn.H.HENENCOURT at 11.30 p.m.

XVII. Lewis Gun limbers will report to their respective Companies about 11 p.m. and will when loaded follow the outgoing Company.

XVIII. Orders re Band have been issued to Q.M. and Bandmaster.

L.P.CAMBIER. Lt.Col.
Comdg 2/10 th Londons.

11.45 p.m. 30/5/18.

HEBUTERNE SECTOR.

SUPPORT BATTALION.

Handing over statement.

2/10th Londons to 8th East Surreys.

I. **Dispositions.** Attached map shows the dispositions of RIGHT FORWARD BATTALION,: LEFT FORWARD BATTALION, and SUPPORT BATTALION'S BATTLE POSITIONS.

Two Companies of the Support Battalion, less two platoons at V.29.a.5.7., are billeted in HEBUTERNE and do not move up to WALLAB Trench as shewn on above mentioned map until they either (i) see the S.O.S. or (ii) receive orders "ATTACK- MOVE" from Battalion Headquarters.

In case of heavy shelling of HEBUTERNE the two rear Companies less two platoons in V.29.a.5.7. are disposed in COURT TRENCH, one on either side of the HEBUTERNE road, and report to Battalion H.Q. when this is done.

II. Battalion Headquarters are in HEBUTERNE V.27.d.7.4. but a dug-out is being made on S.E.side of sunken road at V.29. b.7.5.

This will not be ready until about June 2nd.

There is useful splinter-proof accommodation for a portion of Battalion H.Q in V.29.a.5.7. This has been cleaned for occupation but not used by the Support Battalion. Two platoons will be there tonight to hand over.

III. (a) Plan of HEBUTERNE shewing billets of the 1½ Coys. in HEBUTERNE is attached.

(b) Transport and Q.M.stores at West End BOIS ROBERT BAIZI BUX.

IV. Rations and R.E.material for the forward Companies are dumped by limber at V.30.d.9.5 (or D.6.b.7.5.) according to the area in which R.E.material is required.

V. **WORK.** Work now in progress is as follows :-

(a) Hauling out soil excavated by tunnellers,
(i) at HEBUTERNE CHATEAU 3 8-hour shifts of 16 men
(ii) at M.G. dug-out in the trench occupied by the forward Company 3 8-hour shifts of 6 men.

(i) is found by one of the Companies in HEBUTERNE
(ii) is found by the left forward Company.

(b) 50 men of Right Forward Company deepen and widen the South end of MELBOURNE.

50 men of Left Forward Company deepen and widen VALLEY TRENCH AND BRISBANE TRENCH.

50 men of one of the Companies in HEBUTERNE deepen and widen AUSTRALIAN STREET between JULLEY and VALLEY Trench and make fire bays facing South and facing North (on edge of Terrace)

(c) 10 men of one of the Companies in HEBUTERNE report to R.E.Dump HEBUTERNE CHATEAU at 8-30 p.m. nightly for loading.

VI. Guards are found from one of the Companies in HEBUTERNE as follows :-

VI. Guards.

  S.A.A. Sections at Brigade H.Q. 1 NCO & 5 men
  Wells in MERCOURT ... ... 1 NCO & 5 men
  " " MILLENCOURT ... ... 1 NCO & 5 men

VII. S.A.A. is much below establishment. Deficiencies have been applied for from Brigade

	Establishment.	Actually.
MELBOURNE RIGHT	38,000	7,000
MELBOURNE LEFT	36,000	19,000
WALLABY SOUTH	38,000	30,000
WALLABY NORTH	38,000	30,000
BATTALION RESERVE		
Unfinished H.Q.	20,000	nil
MERCOURT.	20,000	18,000

VIII. Battalion A.A.A.C. Section mounts guns at

  V.30.b.4.6.
  V.30.d.5.9.
  W.25.c.1.6.

Establishment.	Actually.
22 magazines	22 magazines.

B.M.7/75 of 22/5/18 1/4th Inf Bde is attached.

IX Water drawn from wells in MERCOURT and MILLENCOURT required heavy chlorination.

       (signed) E.P.DALSTON.
         Lt.Col.
          Commanding
31st May 1918.   2/10th London Regiment.

 Copy of Commanding Officer
    8th East Surreys
    175th Infantry Brigade

Vol 17

Confidential

2/10th B. Lond. Regt.

War Diary

From 1st Jan to 30 Jan 1918

Army Form C. 2118.

WAR DIARY
or
INTELLIGENCE SUMMARY.
(Erase heading not required.)

Instructions regarding War Diaries and Intelligence Summaries are contained in F. S. Regs., Part II. and the Staff Manual respectively. Title pages will be prepared in manuscript.

Place	Date	Hour	Summary of Events and Information	Remarks and references to Appendices
Bethencourt	June 1		Bn. was relieved on night of 31st/1st by front of Bethencourt. and moved to Camp in front of Bethencourt. Fell kit. stored in reolong	
	2		Church Parade.	
	3		Bn. provided working parties for burying cable in vicinity of Morlog. Specialist training in vicinity of Camp.	
	4		Parties operating in neighbourhood of Bethencourt. Working party of 50 provided for REO for wood on dugouts.	
Moislains-aux-Bois	5th		Moved to Camp in Wood near MOISLAINS-AUX-BOIS	
	6th		Companies training under Company Commanders. Afternoon devoted to Recreation.	
	7th		Company training in Bayonet fighting, Close order drill Visual in morning. Latter taken recruitly completion. Sports in afternoon.	
	8th		Physical training & musketry completion.	
	9th		Church Parade Bathing	
	10th		Bn. moved by bus to BRIQUEMESNIL and occupied billets	

Army Form C. 2118.

WAR DIARY
or
INTELLIGENCE SUMMARY.
(Erase heading not required.)

Instructions regarding War Diaries and Intelligence Summaries are contained in F. S. Regs., Part II. and the Staff Manual respectively. Title pages will be prepared in manuscript.

Places	Date	Hour	Summary of Events and Information	Remarks and references to Appendices
Briquemesnil	June 11th		Practice operations in BRIQUEMESNIL - FLIXECOURT area.	
	12th		Specialist training in morning. Tactical Route march in evening	
	13th		Specialist training in morning. Tactical Route march in evening	
	14th		Specialist training in morning. Tactical Route march in evening	
	15th		Specialist training in morning. Tactical exercise with Infantry	
			Communications in evening	
	16th		Church Parade & Sports	
	17th		Specialist training in morning. Tactical work in afternoon	
	18th		Bde moved by bus to Wood E of MOUFLERS-AUX-BOIS. Batts billeted	
			Bivouaced to MIRVAUX	
	19th		Bde relieved 2/2nd Londons in Support Reserve	
Line	20th		In reserve Carcaillès Val	
	21st		In reserve Carcaillès Val	
	22nd		In reserve Carcaillès Val	
	23rd		In reserve Carcaillès Val	

Army Form C. 2118.

WAR DIARY
or
INTELLIGENCE SUMMARY.
(Erase heading not required.)

Instructions regarding War Diaries and Intelligence Summaries are contained in F. S. Regs., Part II. and the Staff Manual respectively. Title pages will be prepared in manuscript.

Place	Date	Hour	Summary of Events and Information	Remarks and references to Appendices
Line	June			
Front Line	24		Relieved 7/London in front line Casualties Nil	
	25		Situation quiet except for periodical shelling of trenches. A good deal of movement observed in enemy lines. Casualties 1 OR wounded.	
	26		Situation quiet. Much shelling. Enemy T.M's active on front line. Good deal of movement observed in enemy lines. Casualties 1 OR killed 3 wounded	
	27		Situation quiet. Slight shelling of trench system. Much movement seen in behind enemy lines. Casualties Nil	
	28		Hostile artillery active during morning. Rifle Grenades & T.M's front line. Good deal of movement observed in behind enemy lines. Casualties 1 OR wounded	
	29		Situation quiet. Slight shelling of sector & T.M's on front line. Usual movement observed in enemy lines. Casualties 6 OR wounded	
	30		Situation quiet. Slight shelling of sector. T.M's active against front line. Casualties 1 killed 2 OR wounded	

Wauton
Lt Col
Comdg 2/10 London Regt

Confidential

YB 18 125/58

War Diary

No London Regt

Volume VII — Aug 1st — 31st

1918

WAR DIARY or INTELLIGENCE SUMMARY.

Army Form C. 2118.

(Erase heading not required.)

Instructions regarding War Diaries and Intelligence Summaries are contained in F. S. Regs., Part II. and the Staff Manual respectively. Title pages will be prepared in manuscript.

Place	Date	Hour	Summary of Events and Information	Remarks and references to Appendices
Line	July	1st	Battalion in the Line being Left Battalion, Right Brigade, on the right of ALBERT.	
		2nd	Relieved by the 9th Londons and took over Support Line in Devisur Reserve. Casualties 1 O.R. Wounded at Duty.	
		3rd to 5th	In Support. Casualties Nil.	
		6th	On night 6th/7th were relieved by 2/4th Londons and moved to Devisional Reserve at St. LAURENT FARM. Casualties 2 O.R. wounded	
BARLEUX SYSTEM.		7th to 12th	In Divisional Reserve. The Battalion was inspected by F.O.C. Division at 10 a.m. on the 11th.	
Front Line.		12th to 15th	Relieved the 8th Londons on night 12/13th in front line. Casualties 1 killed & 3 wounded on 15th, and 1 killed on 14th.	
"		16th	On night 16th/17th relieved by 12th Londons and moved into Support Line. Casualties 1 O.R. wounded, 2 O.R. wounded at duty.	
Support Line		17th	In Support. Casualties Nil.	
"		18th	In Support. Casualties 2 O.R. wounded.	

WAR DIARY
or
INTELLIGENCE SUMMARY

Army Form C. 2118.

Place	Date	Hour	Summary of Events and Information	Remarks and references to Appendices
Support line	July 19th		In Support. Casualties:- Lieut. G.W. Grannos killed and 1 O.R. and 3 wounded, 4 2 wounded at Duty.	
Front	20th		Relieved the 9th Londons in Right Battalion Sector, Left Brigade	
"	21		Situation normal. Casualties Nil.	
"	22		Situation normal. Casualties 1 O.R. wounded.	
"	23		Situation normal. Casualties 1 O.R. killed.	
"	24th		but Trenches were shelled with Mustard Gas shells from 9-30pm to 10-30 pm and again from 2am to 3am. 25th. Casualties from this Shelling:- Lieut N.B Lindly. 7/Lieut C.W. Crosby. 7/Lieut L Snikham. and 69 O.R. Gared. 1 O.R. wounded. 1 O.R. killed.	
"	25th	10 a.m	Barrage put down by our artillery for operations under taken by the 8th Londons on our Sector. 3 O.R. killed. Casualties 8 O.R. wounded,	
"	26th		Relieved by 7th Londons and moved to BAIZIEUX. Casualties Nil.	
"	27th		Resting.	

WAR DIARY or INTELLIGENCE SUMMARY

Army Form C. 2118.

Place	Date	Hour	Summary of Events and Information	Remarks and references to Appendices
July	28th		Moved from BAIZIEUX to ROUND WOOD.	
	29th		Resting	
	30th		Battalion relieved the 6th Londons in the line, in front of DERNANCOURT. Casualties Nil.	
	31st		Heavy shelling of our trenches by enemy between 10 a.m. and 1.30 p.m. Casualties 5 O.R. killed and 3 O.R. wounded. The Battalion was relieved by the 132nd Battalion, American Regiment.	

Lt. Col.
Comdg. 2/10th London Regt.

175th Bde.

58th Div.

2/10th BATTALION

THE LONDON REGIMENT

AUGUST 1918

Confidential

War Diary

Volume XIII
August 1st —
August 31st
1918

2/10th London Regt.

WAR DIARY
OR
INTELLIGENCE SUMMARY.
(Erase heading not required.)

Army Form C. 2118.

Place	Date	Hour	Summary of Events and Information	Remarks and references to Appendices
August	1st		Divisional Reserve in St. LAURENTS FARM area.	
	2nd		Divisional Reserve. Commanding Officer inspected the Battalion.	
	3rd		Battalion received orders to proceed via HEILLY to valley N.E. of VAUX-SUR-SOMME where it would come under Command of Major chiefly artillery ammunition but owing to great congestion of traffic, chiefly artillery ammunition wagons, only "B" and "C" Companies were able to reach the valley before dawn. Bn. H.Q. and "A" and "D" Companies remaining in HEILLY.	
	4th		In the afternoon orders were received from 174th Bde. to move to a wood West of VAUX, accordingly "B" and "C" Companies were withdrawn from the valley to the wood, while Bn. H.Q. with "A" and "D" Companies remained in HEILLY.	
	5th		The Battalion moved at dusk up to terraces N.E. of VAUX.	
	6th		"A" Company ordered to relieve a Company of the 8th London in the line in front of SAILLY-LE-SEC. At 10 p.m. the Battalion moved up to the line in front of SAILLY-LE-SEC. with Bn. H.Q. on the edge of the village. Casualties 2 O.R. wounded.	

Army Form C. 2118.

WAR DIARY
or
INTELLIGENCE SUMMARY.

(Erase heading not required.)

Place	Date	Hour	Summary of Events and Information	Remarks and references to Appendices
Line.	August	8th	The 58th Division with Australians on Right and 18th Division on its left attacked at 4-20 a.m. This Battalion attacked to the 174th Bde captured SAILLY-LAURETTE, supported by Tanks, Artillery, and machine guns. and by 6-30 a.m. had pushed forward and cleared a Quarry on the East and Sunken road on the North East of the village. By 9-30 a.m. the Battalion had pushed forward a further 1,000 yards. and were forming a commanding position toward MALARD WOOD. Casualties:- Officers, a/Capt. K.S. BOWRON and 2/Lieut. E.H. STRUEBIG killed, and Lieut. J.W. HRIS., 2/Lieut. J.W. CLARK, and 2/Lieut. I.H. SLY wounded. also 2/Lieut. D.G. RITCHIE. Other Ranks:- 14 killed, 74 wounded. 4 missing.	
		9th	At 4-20 p.m. the Battalion pushed forward and took CHIPILLY and established a line well in advance of the village, this line was handed over to the Americans, the Battalion withdrawing to the support positions with Bn. HQ. in CHIPILLY.	
	Cont'd			

Army Form C. 2118.

WAR DIARY
or
INTELLIGENCE SUMMARY.
(Erase heading not required.)

Instructions regarding War Diaries and Intelligence Summaries are contained in F.S. Regs., Part II. and the Staff Manual respectively. Title pages will be prepared in manuscript.

Place	Date	Hour	Summary of Events and Information	Remarks and references to Appendices
Line	August	9th (ct'd)	Casualties:- officers killed. Lieut B.V. Le BRETON, and Lieut. C.J. GREENWOOD, wounded. Lieut S.T. DENHAM, and 2/Lieut C.R. BURTON. Other Ranks killed. 15, wounded. 42.	
"		10th	The morning spent collecting wounded and dead, and clearing streets of CHIPILLY. In the afternoon the Battalion relieved the 131st Americans on the East side of the village. Casualties 1 O.R. wounded.	
"		11th	Battalion relieved by the 131st Americans in the morning and returned to CHIPILLY, rejoining the 145th Brigade in the afternoon, North of MALARD WOOD. Casualties. Lieut. R.M. PARKER wounded and 4 other ranks. Battalion relieved the 5th BERKS. in the MORLANCOURT SECTOR. The estimated number of prisoners captured on the 9th - 11th is 600 and 145 killed.	

Army Form C. 2118.

WAR DIARY
or
INTELLIGENCE SUMMARY.
(Erase heading not required.)

Place	Date	Hour	Summary of Events and Information	Remarks and references to Appendices
August	12th		Bn. moved to BOIS ESCARDONNEUSE.	
	13th		Resting	
	14th		Battalion Parade, and bathing.	
	15th		Brigade Tactical Exercise.	
	16th		Company Training.	
	17th		Battalion inspected by B.G.C. 145th Bde.	
	18th 19th 20th		Company Training and Battalion Drill.	
	21st		Bn. received orders to move early following morning.	
	22nd		Bn. moved to trenches South of MORLANCOURT. Casualties 2 O.R. missing.	
		About 10-30 p.m	Bn. received orders to move to support line in OLD AMIENS Defence Line in front of MORLANCOURT. 145th Infantry Brigade under Command of G.O.C. 47th Division.	

WAR DIARY
INTELLIGENCE SUMMARY

Army Form C. 2118.

Place	Date	Hour	Summary of Events and Information	Remarks and references to Appendices
Support Line	Aug. 23rd	12	Bn. received orders that on night 23rd/24th Aug. 145th Brigade on the right and 140th Brigade (47th Division) on the left will attack. This Battalion being in Brigade reserve. Zero hour 1 a.m. 24th. Casualties 1 Officer + 1 O.R. wounded.	
	24th		Objective gained, being trenches in front of HAPPY VALLEY. Casualties:- Capt. T.B. JACK and Capt. R.J. MARTIN, Lieut H. WOOD and Lieut D.P. HORNE wounded. 26 O.R. Killed, 119 O.R. wounded, L.O.R. missing, and 2 O.R. Gassed.	
	25th		At 2-30 a.m. 145th Brigade attacked being right Brigade with 140th Brigade on left, zero hour being 2-30 a.m. This Bn. as Centre Bn. with 9th Londons on left and 12th Londons on the right. Objective gained by 5-10 a.m. being line running through TRIGGER WOOD in front of BRONFAY FARM with Bn. H.Q at BRONFAY FARM. Between 10 a.m. and noon the 144th Brigade leap-frogged	

WAR DIARY
or
INTELLIGENCE SUMMARY.
(Erase heading not required.)

Army Form C. 2118.

Place	Date	Hour	Summary of Events and Information	Remarks and references to Appendices
Line	Aug. 25th (cont.)		the 145th Brigade and gained objective EAST of BILLON WOOD. Casualties. MAJOR. NICHOLS J. M.C. (Commanding officer), Capt. R. WARD M.C., R.A.M.C., Capt. J.S.T. BERRELL, and 2/Lieut. J.H. BURTON, gassed. 14 O.R. Killed, 55 O.R. wounded, and 20 O.R. Gassed.	
	26th		Bn. withdrew at 1 a.m. to Terraces 2,000 yards S.E. of BRONFAY FARM. Casualties:- Lieut. E.A. HUDSON. Gassed. 2 O.R. Killed 10 O.R. wounded. 5 O.R. missing and 3 O.R. Gassed.	
	27th		Bn. moved about mid-day up to Trenches EAST of BRONFAY WOOD. Casualties 6 O.R. Killed. 6 O.R. wounded, 1 O.R. missing and 3 O.R. Gassed.	
	28th		At 11 p.m. Bn. relieved 7th. Londons in front line S.E. of MARICOURT. Casualties:- 7 O.R. Killed, 28 O.R. wounded 9 O.R. missing, 3 O.R. Gassed.	

WAR DIARY
or
INTELLIGENCE SUMMARY.
(Erase heading not required.)

Army Form C. 2118.

Place	Date	Hour	Summary of Events and Information	Remarks and references to Appendices
France	Aug. 29th		Enemy had retired about 4,000 yards to a position S.E. of MAUREPAS. Bn. advanced to within a distance of 500 yards of the enemy and consolidated. Casualties. 2/Lieut. B. HAZLEDEN and 2/Lieut. P.M. WILHELM wounded. 2 O.R. wounded.	
	30.		Enemy had retired again during night about 4,000 yards to a position WEST of BOUCHAVESNES. At 11-15am Bn. moved forward preceded by the Northumberland Hussars, and took up position WEST of MARRIERES WOOD. Casualties. Lieut. C. IVIMEY (acting Adjutant) Gassed. 2 O.R. Killed and 4 O.R. wounded. 1 O.R. Gassed.	
	31st		Bn. was relieved at 5 p.m. by Bn. of 44th Division and moved back to position S.E. of MARICOURT. Casualties. 1 O.R. wounded.	

M Boyd
Capt.
O.C. 2/10 London Regt.

35807.   W16879/M1879 500,000 3/17 R.T. (1074   Forms W3091/3   Army Form W.3091.

Cover for Documents.

Nature of Enclosures.

2/10th BATTALION, THE LONDON REGIMENT.

SUMMARY OF OPERATIONS.
SAILLY-LAURETTE and CHIPILLY.

August 3rd to 12th 1918.

Lieut.Colonel E.P.Cawston
Commanding 2/10th London Regiment.

Notes, or Letters written.

2/10th BATTALION, LONDON REGIMENT.

SUMMARY of OPPERATIONS.

SAILLY LAURETTE and CHIPILLY.

August 3 to 12 1918.

———oOo———

On the afternoon of 3rd August 1918 the Battalion, which was in bivouacs near ST.LAURENT FARM and under orders to proceed to VIGNACOURT where the Brigade was to be in Corps reserve, received orders from Brigadier General Maxwell Scott temporarily commanding 175.I.B. to proceed via HEILLY to the valley in J.27.a. about 750 yards North East of VAUX-SUR-SOMME where it would come under the command of G.O.C. of 174. I.B. and operate on the morning of the 8th with that Brigade in the impending attack on the German System West and North of SAILLY LAURETTE.

Strict orders were received that the whole success of the operations depended upon the strictest secrecy and that no movement of formed parties was to take place except under cover of darkness.

On arrival of the Battalion at HEILLY it was found that the only road leading from HEILLY to the destination of the Battalion was completely blocked with artillery ammunition wagons and lorries which were establishing an ammunition dump in the ANCRE VALLEY and South of HEILLY; and congestion was becoming more acute as streams of transport entered HEILLY from FRANVILLERS on the North West and from BONNAY on the South West. Two broken down lorries near the narrow and only bridge across the ANCRE, amid general congestion made progress impossible, and as there was no other route to the Battalion's destination other than the circuitous one through BONNAY, which was too lengthy to allow the Battalion reaching its destination before dawn, the

(1).

traffic was picketed and two Companies "B" and "C" dribbled in single file through the traffic to the valley J.27.a.; Battalion H.Q. and "A" and "D" Companies had to remain at HEILLY.

No information was available as to the location of 174.I.B.H.Q., but after tapping a number of gunner wires H.Q. of 58th I.B. 18th Division was located behind the HEILLY CHATEAU. A wire was sent through by them to H.Q. 174.I.B. via 58th Division reporting the situation.

Late on the afternoon of 4th orders were received from 174.I.B. to move to a wood West of VAUX and vacate the bivouacs occupied by "B" and "C" Companies at J.27.a. These two Companies were accordingly withdrawn at dusk and before proceeding to detination Major.J.Nichols.M.C. the Second in Command, rode over to LAHOUSSOYE to confer with the Staff Captain with regard to accommodation and bivouac sheets. As a result of this conference the Battalion remained at HEILLY and the situation was reported to 174.I.B. by wire.

At 11a.m. on the following day the Commanding Officer reported to 174.I.B. at LAHOUSSOYE and received order to move the Battalion to the Terraces J.27.a. at dusk, and that the general attack would take place on the morning of the 8th. The general plan of the attack so far as the 58th Division were concerned is shewn on Map "B" attached. The 174.I.B. to which the 2/10th Londons were attached were to attack the Green Line and at the same time the Australians were to attack on the South of the ANCRE and the 18th Division on the Left of the 174.I.B. with the 12th Division on the Left of the 18th Division. One hour after the capture of the Green Line by the 174.I.B. the 173.I.B. were to advance through 174.I.B. and take the Red Line. The role of the 2/10th Londons was to take and mop up SAILLY LAURETTE and as soon as this

5ᵗʰ Aug

had been done they were to receive orders to withdraw to rejoin the 175.I.B. in Corps Reserve.

Zero hour was 4-20.a.m on 8th instant.

One Company of the 10th was ordered to relieve on the night of the 6th, a Company of the 8th Londons in the trenches astride the SAILLY-LE-SEC- SAILLY-LAURETTE Road with their Right on the Canal Bank. "A" Company (strength two Platoons) was detailed for this.

The Officers with the Battalion at this time were:-

    Lieut.Colonel.E.P.Cawston, 87th.R.I.F. Commanding
    Major.J.Nichols.M.C. 2nd in Command.
    Captain.T.B.Jack, A/Adjutant.
    Lieut.H.Wood. Intelligence Officer.
    Lieut.E.A.Hudson. Signal Officer.
    Lieut.R.J.Martin. Lewis Gun Officer.

"A" Company.

Captain.K.S.Bowron.D.C.M.
Lieut.V.F.Tuffley.
2/Lt.C.J.Greenwood.
" I.H.Sly.

"B" Company.

Captain.E.A.Bye.D.C.M.
Lieut.C.Ivimey.
2/Lt.R.W.Chamberlin.
" R.T.Clemens.

"C" Company.

Lieut.B.V.Le.Breton.
Lieut.J.W.Aris.
Lieut.R.M.Parks
2/Lt.C.A.Burton.
" J.W.Clark.

"D" Company.

Captain.J.S.T.Berrell
2/LT.E.H.Struebig.
" D.G.Ritchie.

Major J.Nichols.M.C. was ordered on the evening of the 7th, to withdraw to Battle Surplus.

The C.O.; 2nd in Command; Intelligence Officer; attached Machine Gun Officer; Company Officers and a number of the Senior N.C.Os reconnoitred the objectives on the 6th and 7th from the Australian Support Line North East of Hamel.

Reconnaissance and study of Aerophotos, Intelligence Reports and liaison with the Australian Brigade led to the conviction that even when the village of SAILLY-LAURETTE had been cleared considerable risk would be ran of the capture not being permanent, unless the Quarry and Spur on the far side of the village were also dealt with and occupation consolidated. These two features appeared to hold enemy local reinforcements and the Quarry had for some days impeded the operations of the Australians. It was accordingly decided that the Battalion would take as its objective the capture and clearing of the village and the subsequent establishment of a line well forward.

The promised assistance by the Tanks who were to take the routes shown on Map "C" and advance with the Infantry at Zero was to have been supplemented by two Platoons of the 175.I.B. working with the Tank "JUTLAND" but in anticipation of a possible hitch 2 Platoons of "D" Company of 2/10th Londons were detailed to co-operate, and Companies were warned that they were not to wait for the Tanks or rely for direction upon their Tanks taking the course indicated.

With reference to the Map "C" attached to Battalion Orders, the Company Colours of the Companies of the Battn are:-

"A" Blue. "B" Yellow. "C" Green. "D" Red.

The routes by which the Companies were to proceed to their objectives are shown in the Company colour on the attached Map "C".

Owing to the dense fog which prevailed at the time none of the three Tanks, upon which Companies had to an extent relied for maintaining direction, started off, until at least 10 minutes after the operations had commenced. The two Platoons of the 173rd.I.B. which were to co-operate were not seen.

Two Eighteen Pounders allotted to the Battn Supplemented the Divisional barrage by enfilading the strongly held sunken road running from the centre of SAILLY-LAURETTE up the centre of the Spur at the North Eastern end of the Village to K.32. central, lifting at zero plus 15 minutes to the Quarry, Terraces and Road leading between the Village and K.32.central.

One Section of Machine Guns under Lieut. Bloomfield were located South of the SAILLY-LE-SEC - SAILLY LAURETTE Road supplemented the barrage of the Eighteen Pounders, and as soon as the Village was captured and the Lines consolidated around the North East of the Village these machine Guns were brought up to the Quarry, two being placed at the Southern edge controlling the Road to CHIPILLY and the slopes on the North of the Road, and two on the North edge controlling the Spur. Both these barrages appear to have been of valuable assistance in hindering local reinforcements.

ASSEMBLY.

The assembling and forming up were organised and carried out as follows:-

"A" (strength 2 Platoons) were holding the Trenches across the LE-SEC-LAURETTE Road, B.C.& D. Companies were bivouaced in the Terraces J.27.a.

At 11.p.m. B.C.& D moved off in that order at intervals of ¼ hour along the LE-SEC-LAURETTE Road, through SAILLY-LE-SEC and on reaching our Front Line at J.35.a.8.8., wheeled to the Left and proceeded N.N.E. behind the Trench, until reaching their jumping off positions. "A" remaining in their previous Trench positions until "D" had passed them and then followed up in rear of "D". This left unprotected the S.E. approaches to SAILLY-LE-SEC. The 174th.I.B. were informed of this fact and approved.

The night became foggy about 1-30.a.m. and by 2.a.m. was very thick. At 3-45.a.m. the Battalion was in position and ready to attack. The fog was dense until 7.a.m.

By 6-30.a.m. not only had the Brigade Orders been carried out and SAILLY-LAURETTE cleared of the enemy (with the exception of two machine gun teams which held out at the Church until cleared with the assistance of a Tank at 7.a.m.) but the Quarry on the East and Sunken Road on the North East of the Village had been captured after considerable resistance and a line established along the Battn Dotted Line indicated on Map "C"; with Battalion H.Q. in the Quarry.

By 9-30.a.m the Battalion had pushed a further 1,000 yards forward and was holding a commanding position well up the Spur towards MALARD WOOD as shown on Map "D" with a half Section of Machine Guns on either flank and four German Machine Guns in the Quarry trained on and ready for operation along the valley towards CHIPILLY.

These were subsequently used and supplemented by Lieut.Bloomfield's Section.

The conservatively estimated number of prisoners captured is about 500 of which 150 were from Western and North Western defences of the Village, 100 from the village, 70 from the Sunken Road defences North East of the Village and 150 from the Quarry.

Over 285 were dealt with at Battalion H.Q. in SAILLY-LE-SEC before 10.a.m.

The estimated number of killed is 150.

PHASE 2.
ADVANCE TOWARDS CHIPILLY.

Late in the afternoon of the 8th instant the Battalion Commander was summoned back to the 174.I.B. H.Q. which was still in the valley North West of SAILLY-LE-SEC and received orders that two Companies of the 2/10th Londons who were supposed to be located on the Green Line K. 33.b., would at 7 o'clock under a creeping barrage of Eighteen Pounders, push forward due East to the side of the CHIPILLY Spur where elements of the 173rd I.B. were supposed to be. The 2/10th Londons were to operate on the right along the valley and clear up CHIPILLY which was believed to be undefended.

The dispositions of two of the Companies of the 2/10th Londons at this time were fortunately well forward, in K.32.a. as shown on Map "D". "C" Right Forward, "B" Left Forward, "A" on the Causeway between SAILLY-LAURETTE and the Canal, and "D" in reserve in the valley about K.31. central. In addition to the Eighteen Pounders barrage, concentration of heavy guns were to bombard CHIPILLY from 7. to 7-30. By 6-30.p.m. O.C. 2/10th Londons had been able to return to the Quarry, and having misgivings as to the information given him with regard to the positions of the elements of the 2/4th which had at that time not consolidated further East than K.33.a. central and in view of the shortness of time and the desire that at any rate one Company might make use of the barrage which was to fall a mile in front of the forward Company, "C" was ordered to push forward along the crest of the Cliff between MALARD WOOD and the valley and to form a defensive flank on the other side of

LES CELESTIN. "B" followed closely behind and
formed a defensive flank facing North East on the
East of "C" while "D" was ordered to push forward
protected form the North and North East by "C" and
"B" and having taken and mopped up CHIPILLY, to
push up the Spur to the East and South East of the
Village. "A" were to follow "D" and remain in reserve
in the MALARD VALLEY just off the Valley Road. The
dispositions on completion of the operations were to
be as shown on Map "D"

A vigorous Machine Gun barrage was maintained
on CHIPILLY by Lieut.Bloomfield's Section operating
the captured German Machine Guns from the Quarry
from 7-30.p.m.

The promptitude shown by o/c "B" resulted in
being able to work forward not far behind the barrage
to within a short distance of their objective, but
the 173 .I.B. elements only emerged about 20 or 30
yards out of the MALARD WOOD in K.31.a. and were
held up by heavy machine gun fire from the Terraces
on the CHIPILLY SPUR before reaching their objective.
"B" were also held up by heavy machine gun fire before
reaching their objective, and consolidated on the Line
marked on the Map "D" protected by "B" and "C" and by
the cliff North of the Road pushed well forward, and
a party of one Platoon under Sergt.Huffey reached the
Farm at the hairpin corner at the North entrance to
the Village and there came under Machine Gun fire
from 3 directions and suffered several casualties,
but the position which they had reached they

maintained until withdrawn at midnight.

Map "D" shows the dispositions of the Battalion at the commencements of these operations, the objectives, and the positions on which the Battalion consolidated at night fall on the 8th instant.

THIRD PHASE.
THE CAPTURE OF CHIPILLY SPUR.

On the morning of the 9th inst; Lieut. S.T. Denham joined the Battalion with a draft of 100 O.R. mostly under 19 years of age.

Soon after mid-day on the 9th of August Orders were received from the 173.I.B. that the Third Londons were to attack from the Green Line with the Red Line as their objective, and that the 2/10th Londons were to follow in close support. The CHIPILLY SPUR was to be heavily bombarded from 4. to 5.p.m.

By 4.p.m. the Companies were assembled about the South West corner in/of the MALARD WOOD with "C" Right Forward, "B" Left Forward, "D" Supporting "C", "A" supporting "B". Officers were informed that in the event of the Companies on the left or high ground being held up by machine gun fire from the terraces on the CHIPILLY SPUR, as was anticipated, they were to consolidate and keep up a vigorous fire on the Spur and Terraces on the West slope of the Spur, while the Right Companies were to work towards the Right and take the Spur from that flank.

The barrage opened at 4.p.m. and as no troops of the 173.I.B. had arrived at the jumping off point by 4-20.p.m and it appeared that the 2/10th Londons were the most forward troops from K.32. to K.34 central an advance was accordingly ordered.

Map "E" shows the dispositions of the Battalion at 4.p.m.

Very heavy machine gun fire was encountered from the Terraces West of the CHIPILLY SPUR as the Battalion advanced through the Wood, and the Left Forward Company

(11)

"B"; Left Support Company "A"; and a portion of the Right
Forward Company "C" found it impossible to advance East
of the Wood, and accordingly consolidated and kept up
a steady fire on their objective. The 173.I.B. had
followed up and were also consolidating on this Line.
The remainder of "C" worked in a South Easterly direction
taking advantage of the cover of the cliff, and here
they were reinforced by "D" Company. News being
received that the troops on the left of the Battalion
were also held up by machine gun fire from The Terraces,
and particularly from the machine gun post under the
clump of trees at K.34.c.9.2, the Battalion
Commander decided to send the Right Support Company
across to the Northern Northern edge of CHIPILLY
to capture the machine gun nest from the South. At
this time it was clear that the machine guns on the
Terraces had seen the troops assembling for this
flank movement and very heavy machine gun fire was
directed at them and the slopes and Road in K.33.d.
and K.33.c.

Having issued orders for the flank movement
the Battalion Commander received orders to report
back to 173.I.B.H.Q. then at K.26.central, and
on calling at Battalion H.Q. in MALARD VALLEY was
informed that the Brigadier had gone forward from
his H.Q.

He accordingly obtained from Colonel Eddy,
Commanding 1st Battalion 131 American Regiment,
the loan of "K" Company of that Battalion to support
the Right Flank movement.

(12).

The American Commander asked that ~~one~~ an Officer of the 2/10th Londons should be detailed to take Command; Lieut. Hudson was detailed for this duty and at 7-30.p.m the Company went forward. At the same time the gunners were informed of the situation and requested to open a barrage on the Machine Gun nests in the Terraces on the West side of CHIPILLY SPUR, and to drop smoke at the South end of CHIPILLY ~~SPUR~~ Village. To this request they responded promptly and effectively. Four machine guns located on the High ground about K.3 2.b. central near Battalion H.Q. also opened a barrage on the Terraces and shortly afterwards Captain Berrell with a handful of men was seen to have dealt with the QUARRY at the North End of CHIPILLY and to be working along the top Terraces towards the nest of machine guns, which had been holding up the advance. This time his party was not only under machine gun fire from the enemy machine guns in the CHIPILLY VALLEY and from the nest under clump of trees which was their objective but the party had worked forward through the smoke barrage faster than was anticipated and having reached the Terrace was receiving casualties from our own machine gun barrage. To indicate the position of his party to the machine gunners and the troops on the West side of the Valley Sgt. Darby, who was one of the party, deliberately stood up and faced the triple machine gun fire and waved his steel helmet on the top of his rifle, thus giving the necessary information and the machine gun barrage ~~lifted~~ lifted right over the CHIPILLY SPUR. The smoke barrage continued in the valley for some time and was an assistance in enabling the Company of Americans and the remainder of "D" Company of 2/10th Londons to follow up in support of Captain Berrell's Advance. Captain Berrell's party

(13).

reached the Clump of trees, capturing 8 guns and 50 prisoners.

He had previously detailed a ½ Platoon to work through the Village and round the South of CHIPILLY SPUR so as to sweep out any elements in that area, he and the rest of his Company pushed forward and formed a Line from East to West across the 85 contour as shown on Map "E" and about 40 minutes afterwards he was joined by the Company of Americans and by elements of the 174th.I.B. who had succeeded in working across the North end of the Valley.

The New Line was then handed over to the Americans and the party withdrew to Support positions on the West slopes of the Spur, about the North end of CHIPILLY and the remaining Companies came forward to that position.

The Battalion was assembled there about midnight, with Battalion H.Q. in CHIPILLY.

The morning of the 10th was spent collecting wounded and dead, clearing up the roads through and accommodation in CHIPILLY and bathing. The Band Marched up from SAILLY-LE-SEC and arrived at CHIPILLY at 11. a.m.

During the afternoon the Battalion relieved the 131st Americans on the East side of CHIPILLY SPUR, and was relieved by that Battalion during the early hours of the 11th and returned on relief to CHIPILLY, rejoining the 175th I.B. in the afternoon in the re-entrant North of MALARD WOOD.

On the night 11th/12th the battalion relieved the
5th BERKS in the MORLANCOURT SECTOR and was relieved
on the following night by the 24th LONDONS (QUEENS).

The estimated number of prisoners captured
in operations against CHIPILLY were 100 and 25 killed.

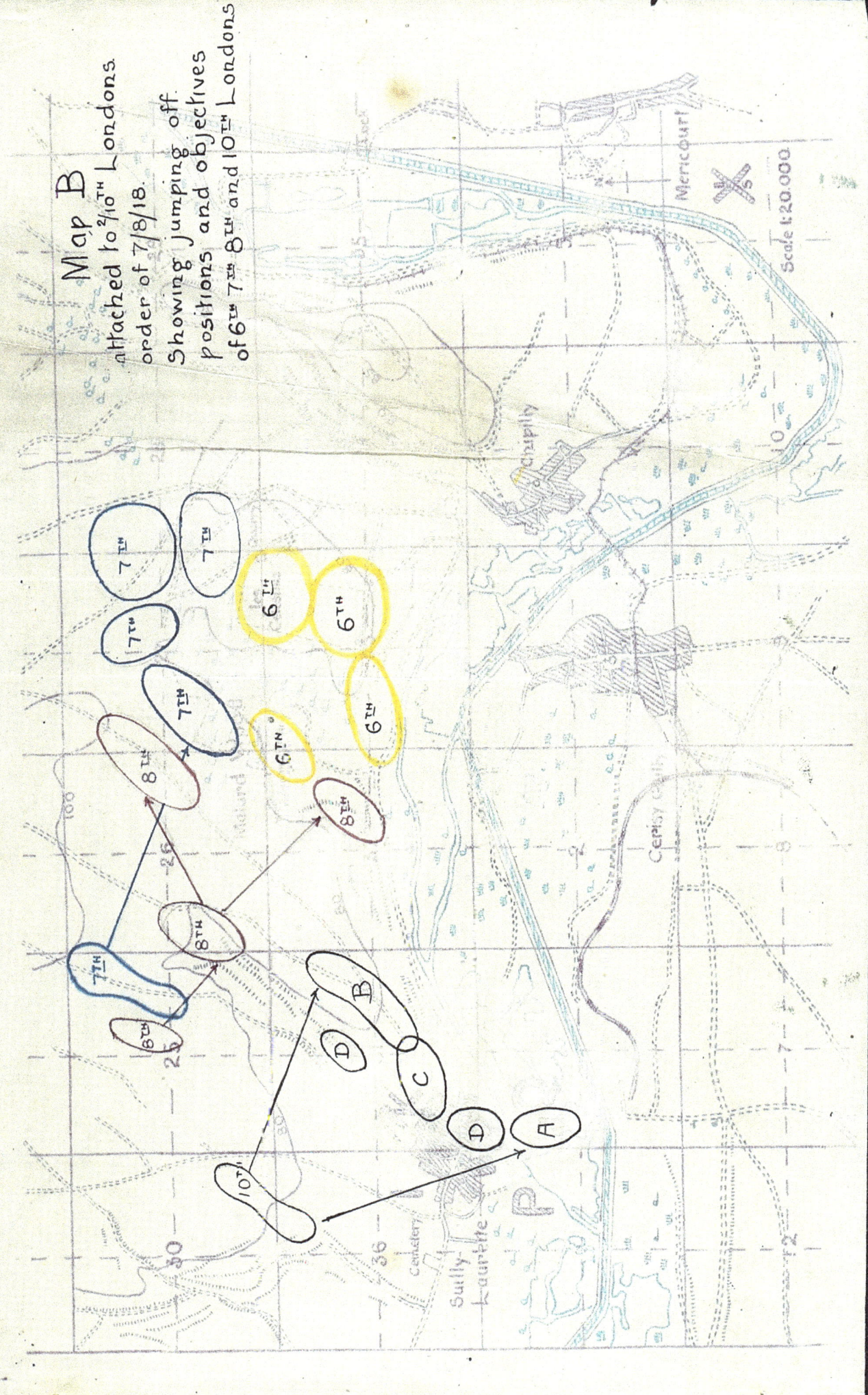

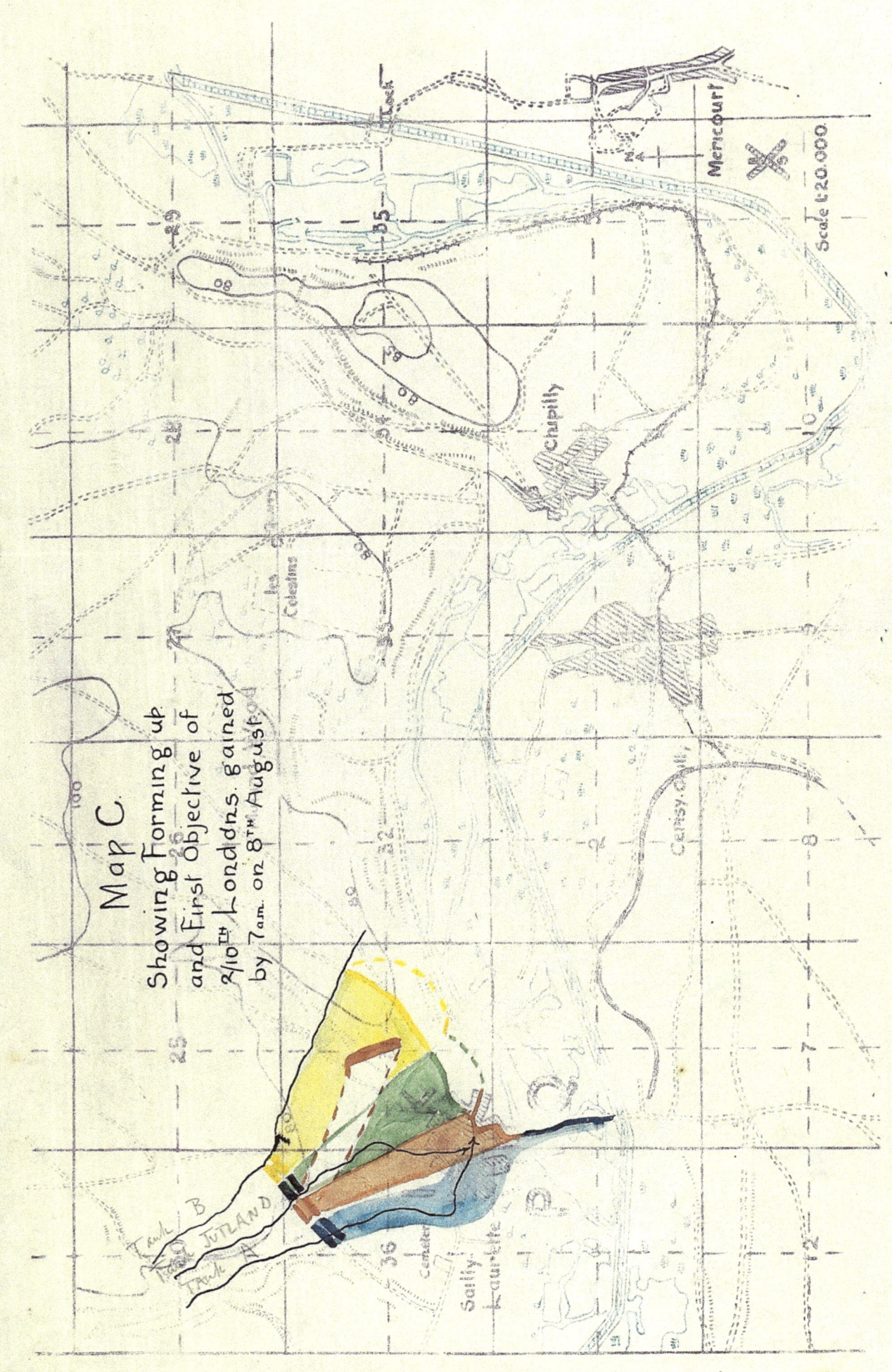

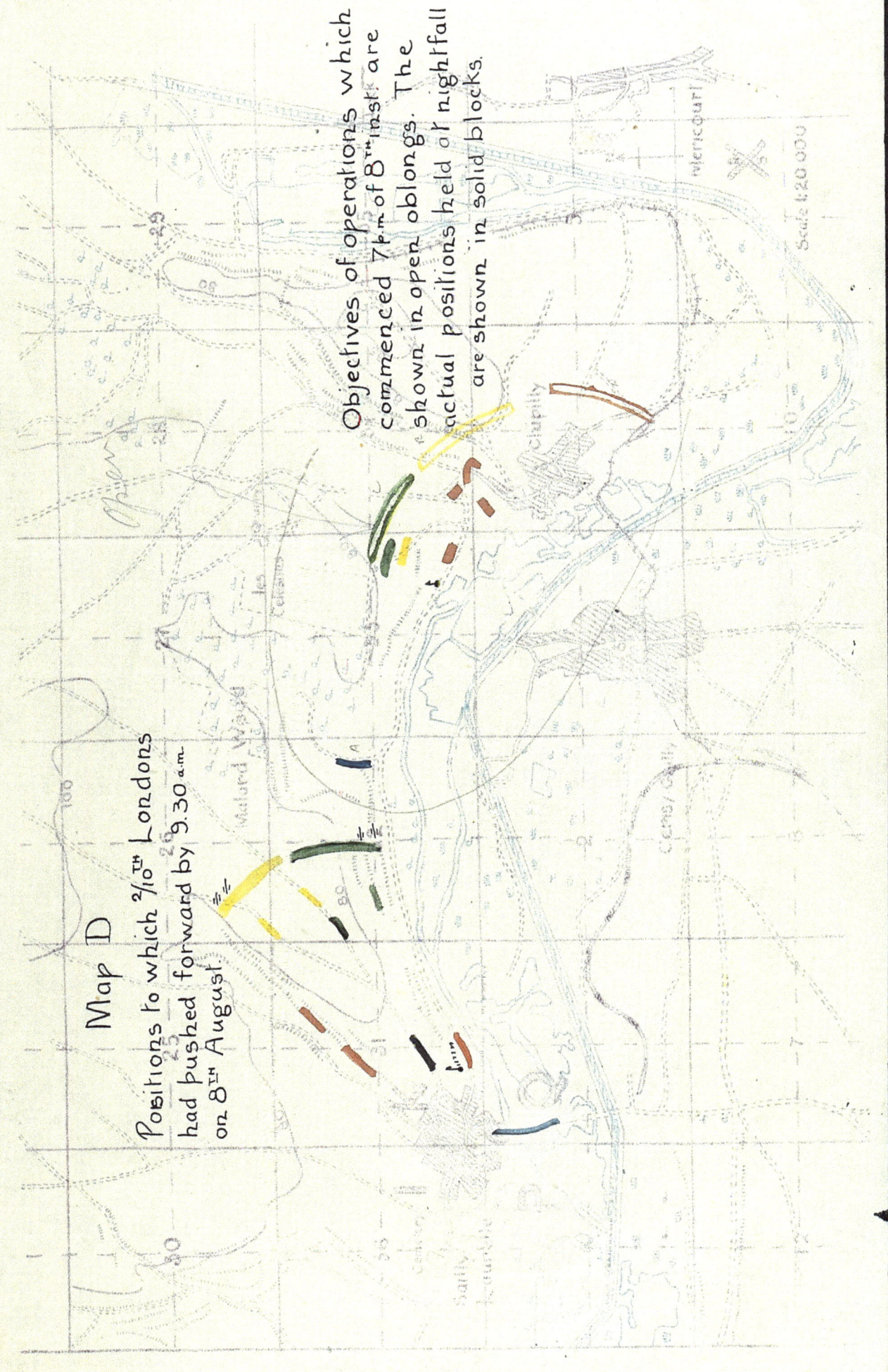

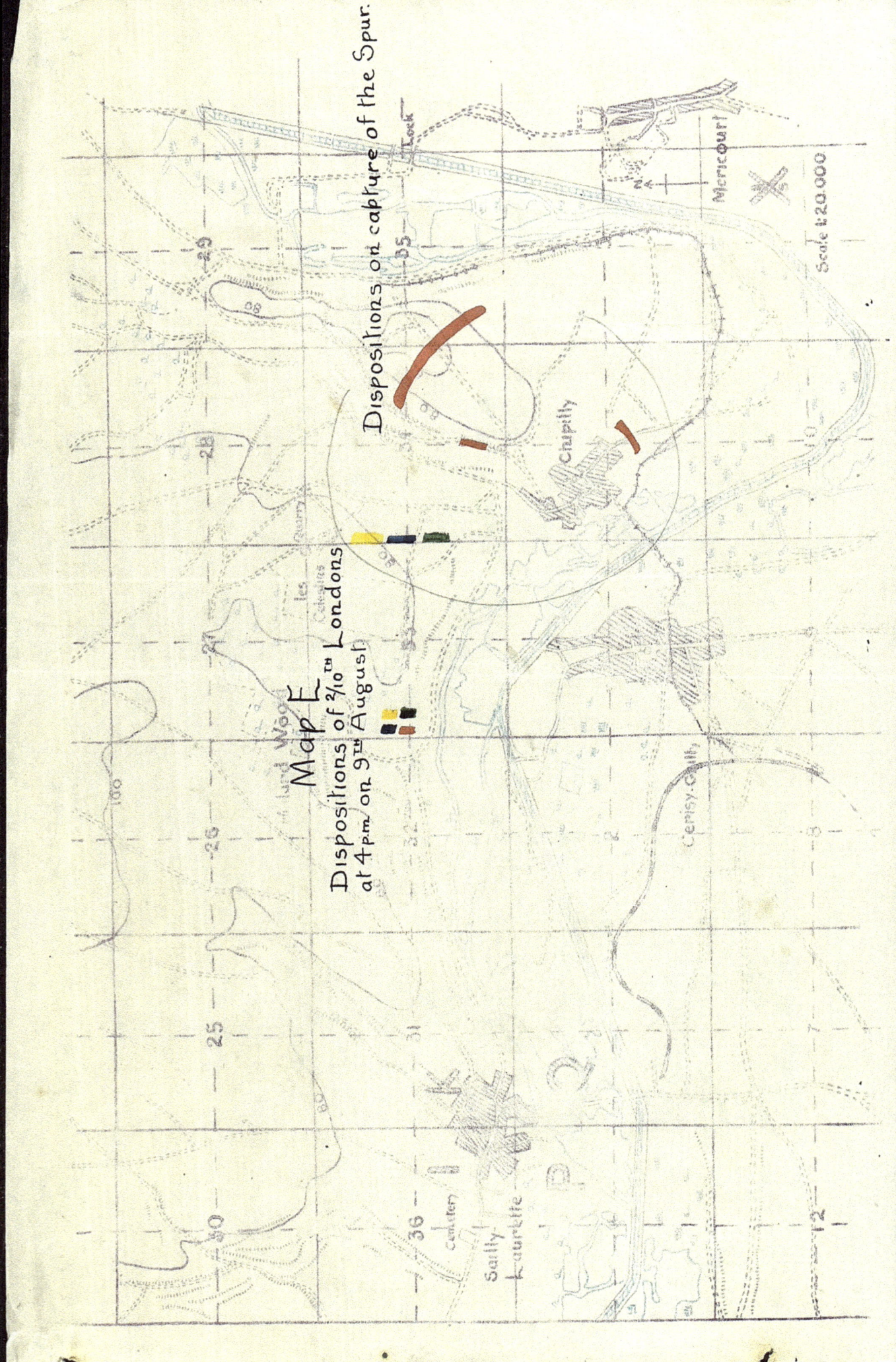

The Battalion Casualties during these operations were:-

Officers. Killed.

Lieut..(A/Capt).K.S.Bowron.
Lieut.B.V.L..Breton.
Lieut.C.J.Greenwood.
2/Lieut.E.H.Struebig.

Officers. Wounded.

Lieut.J.W.Aris.
Lieut.S.T.Denham.
Lieut.R.M.Parker.
2/Lieut.D.G.Ritchie.
" "   J.W.Clark.
" "   I.H.Sly.
" "   C.A.Burton.

Sergeants Killed.

423387. Sgt. Morris.T.
420872. "   Hiffey.L.

Sergeants. Died of wounds.

B201052 Sgt.Wintringham.A.

Sergeants. Wounded.

740906. Sgt.Lindsell.
425328. "   Corck.F.C.
748259. "   Salter.F.
421249. "   Leach.H.
423400. "   Butcher.E.
422303. "   Kitchenmaster.G.
23351.   "   Witherington.F.

Other Ranks. Killed.   2 2

   ditto   Wounded. 148

   ditto   Missing.   4.

   Total Killed. 4 Officers.
                  2 Sergeants.
                 16.Other Ranks.

   Total died of
       wounds.   1.Sergeant.
                 6.Other Ranks.

   Total wounded. 7 Officers.
                   8 Sergeants.
                 148 Other Ranks.

   Total missing. 4. Other ranks.

To,
  Headquarters,
    175th Infantry Brigade.

Herewith Summary of Operations at SAILLY-LAURETTE and CHIPILLY, complete as forwarded to 174th Infantry Brigade, on the 19th instant.

It is regretted you were not furnished with a copy before, owing to the shortage of Maps.

Lieut.Colonel.
Commanding 2/10th London Regiment.

21.8.18.

2/10th. BATTALION.
THE LONDON REGIMENT.

SUMMARY
- of
OPERATIONS.

SAILLY-LAURETTE and CHIPILLY.
———oOo———
August........ to........1918.

Lieut.Colonel.E.P.Cawston.
Commanding 2/10th London Regiment.

August 1918.

The Battalion Orders for the capture of

SAILLY LAURETTE

were as follows:-

I. At ZERO hour, ZERO day, both of which will be notified later, the 58th Division with Australians on Right and 18th Division on its Left will attack.

II. The 174th Infantry Brigade will capture the Green Line on attached Map "B", the 2/10th (attached to 174th Infantry Brigade) will capture SAILLY-LAURETTE.

III. One hour after the capture of the Green Line, the 173rd Infantry Brigade will pass through the 174th Infantry Brigade and capture the Red Line, which is the final objective of the 58th Division.

IV. The attack of the 174th Infantry Brigade will be delivered by the 6th, 7th and 10th Londons, with 8th Londons (less one Company) in Support.
The attack will be supported by Tanks, Artillery and Machine Guns.

V. Battalion Boundaries and dispositions of Units on forming up and on their objectives are shown on Map "B" attached.
The forming up Line is subject to variation according to the tactical situation.

VI. The 10th Londons will capture SAILLY-LAURETTE, exploiting the work of the Tanks in that Village.

VII. The approx. assembly positions and the objectives of Companies are shown on the attached Map "C", each Company being represented by its Company Colour.

VIII. Time by which Companies will be in position in the assembly area and the Line on which they will form up will depend on tactical situation and be notified verbally.

IX. "A" Company preceded by the attached Platoon of "D" on its left will work up along the British Front Line and form up about J.30.d.5.0. to J.36.b.3.9. and will at Zero follow the Tanks which will take route Marked "A" on Map "C".
The Platoon of "D" attached to "A" will, on reaching its assembly position come under command of O.C."D" and with one other Platoon of "D" will at zero work S.E. between the Tank JUTLAND and track "A", joining Jutland Tank at the entrance to the Village.
The remaining Platoons of "D" will follow 50 yards in the rear of "C" and "B" and will mop up the copse K.31.a.5.8. and on reaching K.31.a.central will remain in Support in K.31.central, keeping in touch with the situation of "B"'s Left and in the event of failure on the part of Troops on his Left will form a defensive flank facing N.E. and act on the initiative of O.C."D" to reinforce where most required.
"C" Company will work in conjunction with Tank JUTLAND as far as the North edge of the Village.

X. Platoons working with a Tank must not close round it but will follow it one on either side at a distance of about 30 yards and so as to be able to take advantage of any situation created by the tank.

On arrival in the Village or other obstacle, Tank Platoon Commanders must act on their own initiative and adopt whatever formation is best to kill the garrison and clear the Village.

XI. When the whole of the Village has been thoroughly dealt with and riflemen or Lewis Guns posted to shoot any enemy who have been overlooked and to control all exits, the Tank Platoons of "D" Company will hold the Line Quarry (K.1.c.8.2.) North of Causeway (O.1.a.2.8.) and "A" Company will prolong thence to GAILLY BRIDGE (O1.c.4.7.) at which point the liaison will be established with the 42 Battalion Australians.

XII. O.C."C" Company will when he has established his Green Line push his right flank forward to link up with the Left. "D"'s Tank Platoons at the Quarry and C & B Companies will also co-operate by establishing posts along the Dotted Lines and thus control the Valley.

XIII. During the clearing of the Village "A" will drop 2 Lewis Gun Teams about the Cross Roads J.36.d.2.4. to deal with any opposition from the S.W. corner of the Village.

B. will establish liaison with the 8th Londons (Red on Map "B") or other nearest Troops on his left.

XIV. The Tank following route "B" should be of assistance to O.C."B" but the routes given are liable to be varied and B.& C Companies must keep their own direction.

XV. SIGNALS. Battalion observing Stations will be established about J.28.d. O. 95 and Companies will, if the atmosphere admits use all means of visual signalling to that point.

K.31.central and the TWELVE TREES at K.31.c.5.4. are visible from the Battalion O.P.

Battalion Signalling Sergeant will at once arrange that 2 Signallers per Company see the objectives from this Station and select positions from which to visual.

B.& C. Companies will on having attained their Solid Line, fire the Rocket Triple white from that line and a similar rocket from their Dotted Lines on having established themselves on their Dotted Lines.

O.C.A & D Companies will fire the Rocket Triple White (from the Church) when they are satisfied the Village is clear and a further Rocket when on their Solid Line.

XVI. Battalion H.Q. and R.A.P. will be at J.29.c.5.7.

XVII. Orders with regard to formation of Troops, Tanks Signals, barrage (Artillery and M.G.) equipment, bombs, water, wounded, prisoners, S.A.A. etc., have been issued verbally.

(Sd) E.P.Cawston.
Commanding 2/10th London Regiment.

August 7th 1918.

SUPPLEMENT

to

ORDER for capture of SAILLY LAURETTE.

I. Reference barrage Map shown to all Officers: at Zero Companies will move forward, keeping as close under the creeping barrage as possible.

The barrage moves over the first 400 Yards in 4 minutes and then the next 250 yards in 8 minutes and subsequently at the rate of 100 yards in 4 minutes

II. Two 18 pounders are attached to the 10th Londons and will give enfilade barrage from a position South East of SAILLY-LE-SEC and will fire from zero to zero plus 15, approx, along line K.31.central K.32.a.central and from zero plus 15 to zero plus 30 approx; along line K.31.a.central. K.31.a.central.
They will fire at any enemy on South or South West side of SAILLY-LAURETTE bewteen zero and zero plus 30.
One Section of Machine Gunners will be located at S.W. side of SAILLY-LE-SEC and fire on the same barrage Lines.

III. The 42nd Battalion A.I.F. has as its objective the establishment of a line form the Bridge GAILLY to CERISY GAILLY inclusive.

                                            (Sd).E.P Cawston.
                                            Lieut.Colonel.
Augt.7th 1918.   Commanding 2/10th London Regiment.

To, Headquarters,
    175th Infantry Brigade.

    Reference your B.M.449; narrative re operations
SAILLY-LAURETTE and CHIPILLY were forwarded to 174th Infantry
Brigade; on the 19th instant and their receipt obtained at
10-20.p.m.

                                          Lieut.Colonel.
                                Commanding 2/10th London Regiment.

21.3.18.

Army Form C. 2118.

WAR DIARY
or
INTELLIGENCE SUMMARY.
(Erase heading not required.)

Place	Date	Hour	Summary of Events and Information	Remarks and references to Appendices
September	1918	1st	Bn. cleaning up and reorganization of Companies.	
		2nd	Company Drill, musketry and Arms Drill in the morning with one hours physical drill in the afternoon.	
		3rd	Brigade Exercises from 7-50am to 1pm, later Company games in afternoon and evening.	
		4th	Company Drill etc.	
		5th	do. do.	
		6th	Bn received orders at 1-0 a.m. that the Brigade will relieve a Brigade of the 47th Division in the line on the night 6/7th. Bn. proceeded to line by busses. Marching out strength:- 13 Officers 491 O.R.	
Line		7th	Bn relieved 18th Londons (London Irish) Relief complete about 2am. 10th Buffs of the 12th Division on left and 9th Londons on the right. Orders received from Brigade that the Battalion would attack at 5 a.m. Objective:- line of railway South of EPEHY.	

WAR DIARY
or
INTELLIGENCE SUMMARY.

Army Form C. 2118.

Place	Date	Hour	Summary of Events and Information	Remarks and references to Appendices
Line	Sept. 18		7th (Cont.) "A" "B" & "C" Companies in front line & "D" Coy. in support. Companies moved forward until held up by M.G. fire from GUYENCOURT and SAULCOURT WOOD. After a Shrapnel barrage Bn advanced through SAULCOURT WOOD and SAULCOURT then forced to halt as Bn on left being held up by M.G. fire. Bn consolidated at 3 p.m. Patrols sent out after dusk & were heavily machine gunned from EPEHY. Casualties:- Lieut V.E. Tuffley Died of wounds. Capt. H.C. Stanton 2/Lieut D.C. Hicks, 2/Lieut J.C. Stewart and 2/Lieut C.J. Miller wounded. Other Ranks 32 Killed, 98 wounded, 9 missing and 1 gassed. 8th Bn holding the line. Casualties Nil. 9th Bn relieved by the 6th Londons (174th Brigade) Relief complete by 3 a.m. Bn in Divisional reserve, Eastern outskirts of LIERAMONT. Casualties 1 O.R. Killed.	

WAR DIARY
or
INTELLIGENCE SUMMARY.
(Erase heading not required.)

Army Form C. 2118.

Place	Date	Hour	Summary of Events and Information	Remarks and references to Appendices
	Sept.	10th	Bn cleaned up and re-organized. Casualties NIL.	
		11th	Bn moved up and relieved the 4th Suffolks in the front line. Special Company R.E. discharged gas into EPHEY. Casualties. NIL.	
		12th	Hostile shelling intermittent during day. Ground between our left flank and the 9th Londons patrolled every half hour after dusk. Nil patrol in front. Casualties other ranks 1 Killed, 10 wounded.	
		13th	Hostile shelling intermittent. Patrol of 1 N.C.O. & 6 men pushed forward to enemy wire, were driven back by heavy M.G. fire. The N.C.O. & two men were wounded. A fighting patrol consisting of 2/Lt. R.W. Chamberlin, 1 N.C.O. and 18 O.R. were pushed forward but no enemy were encountered. Casualties: 2/Lt. R.W. Chamberlin killed, 1 wounded and 1 forced. Other ranks:- 1 missing 1 wounded and 1 forced.	

Army Form C. 2118.

WAR DIARY
or
INTELLIGENCE SUMMARY.
(Erase heading not required.)

Instructions regarding War Diaries and Intelligence Summaries are contained in F. S. Regs., Part II. and the Staff Manual respectively. Title pages will be prepared in manuscript.

Place	Date	Hour	Summary of Events and Information	Remarks and references to Appendices
Sun	Sept 14		Nt. 2 a.m. artillery & machine guns played on enemy posts and Special Coy. R.E. fired gas with mortars on these posts. Enemy shelling intermittent during day. Casualties:- Nil	
	15		Bn. relieved by 7th Londons and marched to VILLE WOOD. Casualties:- other ranks, 3 killed, 2 wounded.	
	16		Bn. resting and cleaning up etc. Commanding officer inspected Bn. Casualties Nil.	
	17		Company training and Baths, Transport inspected by the Brigadier. Casualties Nil.	
	18		Battalion left VILLE WOOD and marched to occupy trenches and sunken roads W. of SAULCOURT. - Casualties Nil.	
	19		Battalion remained in position as above - Casualties Nil.	

Army Form C. 2118.

WAR DIARY
or
INTELLIGENCE SUMMARY.
(Erase heading not required.)

Place	Date	Hour	Summary of Events and Information	Remarks and references to Appendices
Line	Sep. 20.		Battalion took up a position in Railway Embankment EAST of EPEHY at 10 p.m. — Casualties NIL.	
	21.		Battalion attacked trench system DADOS LANE + DADOS LOOP.	
			Casualties 2/Lieut. I.H. SLY	
			" R.T. CALLENDER	
			" H. MEARS } wounded	
			" G.W. SMITH	
			" O.L.W. BRETT	
			" J.C. HEROLD — Wounded & Missing.	
			do. Other Ranks 25 killed — 3 missing — 107 wounded	
			1 gassed.	
	22		Battalion held KILDARE AVENUE and was relieved at 11-30 p.m. by one Company of the Berkshires.	
			Casualties 2/Lieut. F.C. BROAD — killed in Action	
			Other ranks. 1 killed in Action	

WAR DIARY
or
INTELLIGENCE SUMMARY.

Army Form C. 2118.

Place	Date	Hour	Summary of Events and Information	Remarks and references to Appendices
	Sept 23		Battalion came out of the line and entrained at 4 am. Casualties NIL	
	24		Battalion arrived at Trones Wood. Casualties NIL	
	25		Battalion at Trones Wood — Cleaning up. Casualties NIL	
	26		Battalion at TRONES WOOD — Company training. Casualties NIL	
	27		Battalion marched to railhead near Dernancourt and entrained at 4.30 pm.	
	28		Battalion arrived at AUBIGNY and detrained at 7.0 am marched to VILLERS-AU-BOIS — billetted in huts	
	29		Battalion at — do. — Company training.	
	30		Battalion entrained and moved to LIEVIN.	

Ernest M Leslie Maj
Lieut - Colonel
Comdg. 2/10 London Regt.

WAR DIARY or INTELLIGENCE SUMMARY.

Army Form C. 2118.

Place	Date	Hour	Summary of Events and Information	Remarks and references to Appendices
LIEVIN.	1918. OCT.	1-2	Battalion at LIEVIN. Company training & Lewis gun firing. Casualties NIL.	
		2	Lecture to all Officers, W.O.s & N.C.O.s by D.C.O. – Casualties NIL.	
		3	Company training. All Companies received instruction in Anti-gas precautions from D.G.O. – Casualties NIL.	
		4	Company training. Clearing up & improvement of the Town of LIEVIN carried out in the afternoon. – Casualties NIL.	
		5	Battalion employed in mending roads W. of LENS. – Casualties NIL.	
		6	Commanding Officer inspected the Battalion. Company drill. – Casualties NIL.	
		7	Companies at disposal of O/C Companies for training. Commanding Officer, Adjutant & Company Commanders visited Battalion & Company Headquarters of the 7th Batt. London Regt. & reconnoitred the line in the ANNAY Sector. – Casualties NIL.	

WAR DIARY
INTELLIGENCE SUMMARY.
(Erase heading not required.)

Army Form C. 2118.

Place	Date	Hour	Summary of Events and Information	Remarks and references to Appendices
Line	1918 OCT 8		The Battalion relieved the 9th Battalion London Regiment in the ANNAY Sector (night of 8th/9th). "B"+"D" Companies being disposed in front line, "A" Coy. in support & "C" Coy. in reserve - Casualties NIL.	
	9		Situation quiet. Intermittent gas shelling, increased at night. Casualty. 1 O.R. wounded.	
	10		Work improving positions & active patrolling. Intermittent gas shelling at night. Casualties 2/LIEUT. E.A. ENNIS gased. Killed in action 2 O.R. wounded 1 O.R.	
	11		Work improving positions & active patrolling. Intermittent gas shelling at night. Casualties NIL	
	12		The Battalion attacked and took the Village of ANNAY. Casualties. 2/LIEUT. W.H. KNOX Connersion. Killed in Action 1 O.R. wounded 1 O.R. wounded 6 O.R. gased 16 O.R.	
	13		Battalion was relieved in the Line & withdrawn into Reserve. Casualties NIL.	

WAR DIARY or INTELLIGENCE SUMMARY

Army Form C. 2118.

Place	Date 1918	Hour	Summary of Events and Information	Remarks and references to Appendices
Mapshut AA	OCT. 14		Battalion marched to FOUQUIERES where it was billetted - Casualties NIL.	
	15		Company training in FOUQUIERES. - Casualties NIL.	
	16		Battalion marched to COURRIERES leaving the starting point FOUQUIERES CHURCH at 9am route being FOUQUIERES CHURCH, O.21.C.9.9, O.15.d.5.2, O.10.C.7.0, HARNES STATION, O.9.b.7.7, O.5.a.5.5. On arrival Battalion was billetted in the Town of COURRIERES, Battalion H.Q. being opposite the Church. (Map Sheet 44a. 40,000) Casualty 2/LIEUT. J.B. JOHNSTON - Gassed. CAPT. E.H. BYE assumed duties as temporary 2ⁿᵈ in Command of 2/2ⁿᵈ London Regiment.	
	17		Company training at COURRIERES. Casualties NIL.	
	18		The Battalion continued the advance at the head of the Main Body, leaving the starting point P.6.d.7.7 at 07.40 hrs route to being OSTRICOURT - LE FOREST - MONCHEUX - K.36. d. 2.8 - L.31. B.c.6 - RUE COLLETTE - VACQUERIE, where the Battalion spent the night in billets. Casualties NIL.	

Army Form C. 2118.

WAR DIARY
or
INTELLIGENCE SUMMARY.
(Erase heading not required.)

Instructions regarding War Diaries and Intelligence Summaries are contained in F. S. Regs., Part II. and the Staff Manual respectively. Title pages will be prepared in manuscript.

Place	Date	Hour	Summary of Events and Information	Remarks and references to Appendices
Map Sheet 44	Oct. 1918	19	The Battalion marched from VACQUERIE forming the Advance Guard to the Brigade. Battalion advanced in two Columns. "A" & "B" Companies forming the SOUTHERN Column & following the Route PT. DE BEUVRY - BRODERIE - L.35.d.1.8 - L.29.b.4.2 - HEM - AUCHY. "C" & "D" Companies (Map Sheet 44) forming NORTHERN Column & following the Route BRODERIE - LA CARDONNERIE - CHÊNE - DEREGNAUCOURT - AUCHY. Casualty 1 O.R. killed in action.	
		20	The Battalion continued the advance marching in rear of the main body in front of 291 Brigade Artillery, route being NOMAIN - H.Q. a.09. - PLACE MARTIN to AIX where the Battalion was billetted for the night. - Casualties Nil.	
		21	Advanced continued the Battalion marching in rear of Brigade H.Q. in the main body. The route followed was PLACE MARTIN - BELZANDSEE - RUMEGIES, crossing bridge at PONT CAILLOU at 13.00 hours. Battalion H.Q. was established I.11.d.4.2. "C" & "D" Companies being disposed	

WAR DIARY
or
INTELLIGENCE SUMMARY.

(Erase heading not required.)

Army Form C. 2118.

Place	Date 1918	Hour	Summary of Events and Information	Remarks and references to Appendices
	OCT 21 (Contd.)		in the neighbourhood of PONT CAILLOU, "A" & "B" Companies in RUE DOMBRIE. Casualties Nil.	
	22.		Battalion H.Q. moved forward to QUESNOY I.11.C.Central. (Sheet 4H) Casualties Nil.	
	22/23		The Battalion relieved all troops of the 12th Londons on the outpost line S. & E. & W. grid line through I.11.12 Central. "C" Company took over the outpost line. "B" Coy relieved "B" Coy of 12th Londons in CENSE DE CHOQUES. "A" Coy. took over dispositions of "A" Company 12th Londons in RUE DOMBRIE "C" & "D" Companies took over dispositions from 12th Londons at I.K. a. & 6 respectively. Batt. H.Q. remained at I.11.C. Central (Map sheet 4H) & I.9.d.9.1. respectively. Casualties Nil.	

Army Form C. 2118.

WAR DIARY
or
INTELLIGENCE SUMMARY.
(Erase heading not required.)

Instructions regarding War Diaries and Intelligence Summaries are contained in F. S. Regs., Part II. and the Staff Manual respectively. Title pages will be prepared in manuscript.

Place	Date	Hour	Summary of Events and Information	Remarks and references to Appendices
	1918 Oct. 24		Battalion in same position. Casualties 2/Lt. J.J. SHORT gassed, 7 O.R. Wounded, 1 S.O.R. gassed.	
	25		Battalion Headquarters moved to CENSE de CHOQUES during night 25/26. Very active patrolling took place, posts established forward. Casualties NIL.	
	26		FORT MAULDE taken. A & C. Companies advanced & established Headquarters in TRINQUETTE J.8.B. and ROUGE PORTE V.9.C. respectively. (Refce. Map Sheet 44). Casualties NIL.	

Army Form C. 2118.

WAR DIARY
or
INTELLIGENCE SUMMARY.
(Erase heading not required.)

Place	Date 1916	Hour	Summary of Events and Information	Remarks and references to Appendices
	Oct.	27	The Battalion was relieved by 9th London Regiment in the outpost line. All Companies on relief proceeded to billets in RUMEGIES arriving there about 22.00 hours. Casualty 1. O.R. Wounded	
		28	Inspection of Companies by Company Commanders and making up of deficiencies. - Casualties NIL.	
		29-30	Company and specialist training - Casualties - Casualties NIL.	
		31	Battalion practice operations over ground N.W. of RUMEGIES	

George M MacKellkeys
for Lieut-Colonel
Comdg. 2/10 Lond. Regt.

WAR DIARY or **INTELLIGENCE SUMMARY.**

Army Form C. 2118.

Place	Date	Hour	Summary of Events and Information	Remarks and references to Appendices
	1918 November			
	1		Battalion at Rumegies. – Commanding Officer's Inspection.	
	2		Do. Brigade Ceremonial Parade.	
	3		Do. Divisional Church Parade at PLANARD.	
	4		Do. Specialist Training.	
	5		Do. Platoon and Company Training. Firing on Range.	
	6		Do. Company Training, and Practice Tactical Operations.	
	7		Do. Company Training and Bathing.	
	8		Battalion moved forward to MAULDE at 2.30 p.m. 16 Officers + 44 O.R. Transport lines remained at RUMEGIES. Barracks Nil.	
	9		Battalion moved to PERUWELZ via WIERS at head of Main Body behind Brigade Headquarters and 503 Field & 6 Th R.E. Barracks Nil.	
	10		Battalion moved to NEUFMAISON at head of Main Body. Barracks Nil.	
	11		Battalion at NEUFMAISON. Armistice commenced at 11 a.m. Barracks Nil. Band played National Anthems in Village Square.	

Army Form C. 2118.

WAR DIARY
or
INTELLIGENCE SUMMARY.
(Erase heading not required.)

Place	Date	Hour	Summary of Events and Information	Remarks and references to Appendices
	1918 November 12		Battalion at NEUFMAISON. Thanksgiving Service. Games in the afternoon.	
	13		Do. "B" Coy commanded by 2/Lt. J. THORNTON took over the duties of the 12th LONDONS in the Outpost line. Infantry Training. Bayonet Fighting. Field Exercises. Games in afternoon.	
	14		Do. Company Training in morning. Games in afternoon.	
	15		Do. Infantry Training in morning. Games & Cross Country Race in afternoon.	
	16		Do. Commanding Officer's Inspection in morning. Boxing Tournament in afternoon.	
	17		Do. Voluntary Church Service at NEUFMAISON. "Te Deum" for R.C. at STAMBRUGES.	
	18		Battalion moved to STAMBRUGES. Company towards in Evening.	
	19		Battalion at STAMBRUGES. Company Training.	

Army Form C. 2118.

WAR DIARY
or
INTELLIGENCE SUMMARY.
(Erase heading not required.)

Instructions regarding War Diaries and Intelligence Summaries are contained in F. S. Regs., Part II. and the Staff Manual respectively. Title pages will be prepared in manuscript.

Place	Date	Hour	Summary of Events and Information	Remarks and references to Appendices
	1918			
Battalion at STAMBRUGES	November 20		Bathing Parades.	
Do.	21		Brigade Ceremonial Parade in morning. Games in afternoon.	
Do.	22		Military Education & Recreational Training. Same	
Do.	23		Company Training in morning. Games in afternoon.	
Do.	24		noon. Battalion Sports in evening. Church Parade in morning. Games in afternoon.	
Do.	25		Massed Bands of Brigade at Retreat. Military, Educational & Recreational Training	
Do.	26		- Do - Brigade Dinner in evening	
Do.	27		- Do - Battalion Concert in evening	
Do.	28		- Do - 1 Coy Concert in evening	
Do.	29		Military, Educational & Recreational Training. Dance for French Soldiers in evening.	
Do.	30		Div: Ceremonial Parade Rehearsal. Educational and Recreational Training	

Guy M. Mitchell
Major for Lieut. Colonel
London 2/10th LONDON REGT.

Army Form C. 2118.

WAR DIARY
or
INTELLIGENCE SUMMARY.
(Erase heading not required.)

2/10 London Regt Vol 23

Instructions regarding War Diaries and Intelligence Summaries are contained in F.S. Regs., Part II. and the Staff Manual respectively. Title pages will be prepared in manuscript.

Place	Date	Hour	Summary of Events and Information	Remarks and references to Appendices
STAMBRUGES	1918 Decr. 1		Battalion at STAMBRUGES. Lt.-Col. E.P. CAWSTON proceeded on leave. Battalion under the Command of MAJOR G.F. ROTHSCHILD. M.C.	
	2		Church Parade. Inspection by 1st Army Commander.	
	3 & 4		Military, Educational & recreational training.	
	5		H.M. KING GEORGE V accompanied by H.R.H. THE PRINCE OF WALES & H.R.H. PRINCE ALBERT visited the Village & inspected all the Brigade Troops. N.C.O's Dance in evening.	
	6		Military, educational & recreational training. Privates Dance in evening.	

WAR DIARY or INTELLIGENCE SUMMARY.

Army Form C. 2118.

Place	Date	Hour	Summary of Events and Information	Remarks and references to Appendices
STAMBRUGES	1918 Dec. 7		Battalion at STAMBRUGES. Battalion Route March.	
	8		Do. — Church Parade.	
	9		Do. — Military educational & recreational training. Debate in Theatre in evening.	
	10		Do. — Military, educational & recreational training.	
	11		Do. — Bal Masqué in evening. Training in Billets during day owing to wet weather.	
	12		Do. — Battn Parades. Lecture & Brigade	
	13		Do. — Whist Drive in evening.	
	14		Do. — Military, educational & recreational training. Battalion Route March.	
	15		Do. — Brigade Concert in evening. Church Parade.	

Army Form C. 2118.

WAR DIARY
or
INTELLIGENCE SUMMARY.
(Erase heading not required.)

Place	Date	Hour	Summary of Events and Information	Remarks and references to Appendices
STAMBRUGES	1918 Dec 16		Battalion at STAMBRUGES. Military, educational & recreational training.	
	17		Do. Advance party proceeded to LEUZE	
	18		Do. Military, educational & recreational training	
	19		Do. Gymkhana & fancy dress ball in evening. Military, educational & recreational training.	
	20		Do. Battalion parades. Officers bal masque in the evening.	
LEUZE	21		Battalion at LEUZE. Military, educational & recreational training.	
	22		Do. Church Parade.	
	23-24		Do. Military, educational & recreational training.	
	25		Do. Xmas Day. Church Parade.	

Army Form C. 2118.

WAR DIARY
or
INTELLIGENCE SUMMARY.
(Erase heading not required.)

Place	Date	Hour	Summary of Events and Information	Remarks and references to Appendices
LEUZE	1918 Decr. 26		Battalion at LEUZE. Recreational training & games	
	" 27		Do. Military, educational & recreational training. Lecture & N.C.O.s Dance in evening	
	" 28		Do. Bathing parade	
	" 29		Do. Church Parade. Battalion addressed by 12th Battalion of Bryant Sutro.	
	" 30		Do. Military. Educational & recreational training. Officers Dance in the evening	
	" 31		Do. Bathers parade for other Ranks who did not take on the 28th. Military. Educational & recreational training. Brigade Torch Light Tattoo 9.30 pm – 10 pm.	

E Warlow
Lieut. Colonel
Comdg 2/10th London Regt.

WAR DIARY
or
INTELLIGENCE SUMMARY.
(Erase heading not required.)

Army Form C. 2118.

2/10 London Regt.

Place	Date	Hour	Summary of Events and Information	Remarks and references to Appendices
LEUZE.	1919. Jan. 1st.		Battalion at LEUZE. Military Educational & Recreational Training. Battalion Dance in the evening.	
	2nd		ditto. Battalion Route March. Q.V.R.Concert Party "THE QUAVERS" performed to the 2/10th Bn. in the evening.	
	3rd		ditto. Company Training under Os.C. Companies. Boxing Tournament in the afternoon.	
	4th		ditto. Company kit inspection. Lecture on the science of boxing by Major Delaney. League Football Match in the afternoon - 2/10th Bn. v. 512nd Company A.S.C.	
	5th		ditto. Church Parade.	
	6th		ditto. Military Educational & Recreational Training.	
	7th		ditto. Military Educational & Recreational Training. Battalion Sports in the afternoon. Battalion Dance in the evening.	
	8th		ditto. Battalion Route March. Brigade Officers Dance in the evening.	
	9th		ditto. Military Educational & Recreational Training. Inter-Company Football in the afternoon.	
	10th		ditto. Military Educational & Recreational Training.	
	11th		ditto. Inclement Weather. Company Training in billets. Inter-Company Football in the afternoon.	
	12th		ditto. Battalion took over Brigade Duties from the 9th Battalion. Church Parade. Battalion Whist Drive in the evening.	

Army Form C. 2118.

WAR DIARY
or
INTELLIGENCE SUMMARY.
(Erase heading not required.)

Instructions regarding War Diaries and Intelligence Summaries are contained in F. S. Regs., Part II. and the Staff Manual respectively. Title pages will be prepared in manuscript.

Place	Date	Hour	Summary of Events and Information	Remarks and references to Appendices
LEUZE (Cont)	1919 Jan. 13th		Battalion at LEUZE. Military Educational & Recreational Training. Battalion Boxing in the afternoon. I Corps Concert Party "THE VERY LIGHTS" performed to the 2/10th Bn. in the evening.	
	14th		ditto. Military Educational & Recreational Training. Inter-Company Football in the afternoon and Brigade Relay Races. Battalion Dance in the evening.	
	15th		ditto. Battalion Route March. Brigade Officers Dance in the evening.	
	16th		ditto. Military Educational & Recreational Training. Brigade Boxing Contests in the afternoon.	
	17th		ditto. Military Educational & Recreational Training. Brigade Boxing Final in the afternoon and evening.	
	18th		ditto. Companies at disposal of Os.C. Companies. Company bathing.	
	19th		ditto. Battalion relieved by 12th Bn. of Brigade Duties. Church Parade.	
	20th		ditto. Military Educational & Recreational Training. Brigade Tug of War.	
	21st		ditto. Military Educational & Recreational Training. Brigade Cross Country Run. Battalion Dance in the evening.	

Army Form C. 2118.

WAR DIARY
or
INTELLIGENCE SUMMARY.
(Erase heading not required.)

Instructions regarding War Diaries and Intelligence Summaries are contained in F. S. Regs., Part II. and the Staff Manual respectively. Title pages will be prepared in manuscript.

Place	Date	Hour	Summary of Events and Information	Remarks and references to Appendices
LEUZE.	Jany. 22nd		Battalion at LEUZE. Battalion Route March. Brigade Football Final Q.V.R. v. 2/10th result, Q.V.R. 3. 2/10th 0.	
	23rd		ditto. Brigadier's Inspection in the morning. Corps Commander visited the Battalion Area in the afternoon. Battalion Tug of War Teams represented the Brigade in the Divisional Competition in the afternoon.	
	24th		ditto. Military Educational & Recreational Training. Battalion Dance in the evening.	
	25th		ditto. Battalion Route March. Football in the afternoon, 2/10th v. 512th Coy. A.S.C.	
	26th		ditto. Church Parade.	
	27th		ditto. Companies at disposal of Os.C. Companies until 1100 hours to clear away snow from the streets. *Educational Classes after 1100"*	
	28th		ditto. Military Educational & Recreational Training. Battalion Dance in the evening.	
	29th		ditto. Company bathing parades.	
	30th		ditto. Battalion Practice Ceremonial Parade.	
	31st		ditto. Military Educational & Recreational Training.	

E. Cawstone
Lieut.-Colonel,
Commanding 2/10th Battalion The London Regiment.

2/10 London Vol 9

WAR DIARY
or
INTELLIGENCE SUMMARY.

Army Form C. 2118.

Place	Date	Hour	Summary of Events and Information	Remarks and references to Appendices
LEUZE	17-24th		Commanding Officer inspected A & B drafts for Army of Occupation at 1000 hrs in Hackney Empire. Bypass at 1600 hrs next France	
	18th		Embarked at 06 Companies dispersed	
	19th		Draft A paraded and with 100th Rif Post & others. Draft B made Pre Officer	
	20th		Drafts were Roll'n A draft 6 to 16 KRRC B draft 27 & 26 surrender of	
	21st		Army of Occupation OR to Fight Londons	
	22nd		All remaining OR in Batln. form HQ Coy	
	23rd		Company parades at 0900 hrs for fatigues etc	
	24th		Company parades at 0900 hrs for fatigues etc	
	25th		Company parades at 0900 hrs for fatigues etc	
	26th		Company parades at 0900 hrs for fatigues etc	
	27th		Company parades at 0900 hrs for fatigues etc	
	28th		Company parades at 0900 hrs for fatigues etc	

Wimber. Lieut-Colonel.
Comdg. 2/10th Bn London Regt.

To:
   58th Divl. Bde. Group.

   Herewith War-Diary
of this Unit for the Month of
March. Please.

                              [signature]
                              2 Lieut. & a/adjt.
31-3-19   2/10th Bn London Regt.

WAR DIARY or INTELLIGENCE SUMMARY.

Army Form C. 2118.

Place	Date	Hour	Summary of Events and Information	Remarks and references to Appendices
LEUZE	1919 MARCH 1		Battalion at Leuze. Company at disposal of O.C. Company for duties etc	
	2		" Company at disposal of O.C. Company for duties etc	
	3		" Company at disposal of O.C. Company for duties & fatigues	
	4		" Company at disposal of O.C. Company for duties & fatigues	
	5		" Company at disposal of O.C. Company for duties & fatigues	
	6		" Company at disposal of O.C. Company for duties & fatigues	
	7		" Company at disposal of O.C. Company for duties & fatigues	
	8		" Company at disposal of O.C. Company for duties & fatigues	
	9		" Company at disposal of O.C. Company for duties & fatigues	
	10		" Company at disposal of O.C. Company for duties & fatigues	
	11		" Company at disposal of O.C. Company for duties & fatigues	
	12		" Company at disposal of O.C. Company for duties & fatigues	
	13		" Company at disposal of O.C. Company for duties & fatigues	

Army Form C. 2118.

WAR DIARY
or
INTELLIGENCE SUMMARY.

(Erase heading not required.)

Place	Date 1919	Hour	Summary of Events and Information	Remarks and references to Appendices
LEUZE.	MARCH 14		Company at disposal of O.C. Company for fatigues etc.	
	15		Company at disposal of O.C. Company for fatigues etc.	
	16		Company at disposal of O.C. Company for fatigues etc.	
	17		Company at disposal of O.C. Company for fatigues etc.	
	18		Company at disposal of O.C. Company for fatigues. Baths	
	19		Company at disposal of O.C. Company for fatigues etc.	
	20		Company at disposal of O.C. Company for fatigues etc.	
	21		Company at disposal of O.C. Company for fatigues etc.	
	22		Company at disposal of O.C. Company for fatigues etc.	
	23		Company at disposal of O.C. Company for fatigues etc.	
	24		Company at disposal of O.C. Company for fatigues etc.	
	25		Company at disposal of O.C. Company for fatigues etc.	
	26		Company at disposal of O.C. Company for fatigues etc.	
	27		Company at disposal of O.C. Company for fatigues etc.	
	28		Company at disposal of O.C. Company for fatigues etc.	
	29		Company at disposal of O.C. Company for fatigues etc. Baths	
	30		Company at disposal of O.C. Company for fatigues etc.	
	31		Company at disposal of O.C. Company for fatigues etc.	

www.ingramcontent.com/pod-product-compliance
Lightning Source LLC
Chambersburg PA
CBHW081404160426
43193CB00013B/2105